AN HERALDIC ALPHABET

Also by John Brooke-Little

Royal London
Pictorial History of Oxford
Boutell's Heraldry
Knights of the Middle Ages
Prince of Wales
Fox-Davies' Complete Guide to Heraldry

J. P. Brooke-Little

M.V.O., M.A., F.S.A., F.H.S.

RICHMOND HERALD OF ARMS

AN HERALDIC
ALPHABET

New and Revised Edition

ARCO PUBLISHING COMPANY, INC.
New York

Published in the U.S. by
Arco Publishing Company, Inc.
219 Park Avenue South, New York, N.Y. 10003

Copyright © John Brooke-Little, 1973
New and revised edition, 1975
First published in Great Britain in 1973 by
Macdonald and Company (Publishers) Ltd.

Library of Congress Catalog Card Number 72-95468

ISBN 0-668-002941-2

printed in Great Britain

CONTENTS

Author's Forewords ix, xi

1 Heralds and the birth of heraldry 1

2 The development of arms 11

3 The grammar of heraldry 18

4 The law of arms 26

5 The alphabet 30

ILLUSTRATIONS

Opposite page 20
Sir Geoffrey Luttrell
(after the illumination in the Luttrell Psalter)

Opposite page 21
A herald in his tabard

Opposite page 52
Achievement of the arms of Major-General,
the Viscount Monckton of Brenchley, C.B., O.B.E., M.C.

Opposite page 53
The marshalling of arms

The line illustrations are by Mr. Norman
Manwaring, Herald Painter at the
College of Arms, and Miss Alison Urwick.
The coloured illustrations are by
Mr. Robert Parsons, Herald Painter at the
College of Arms.

FOR MARY

FOREWORD

A number of heraldic dictionaries, glossaries and alphabets has appeared over the years and it may seem strange that I have elected to augment it. The reason is that I have attempted to do it in a rather different way.

In the first place, I have prefaced the actual Alphabet with an essay on heraldry, as seen through the eyes of a herald, rather than purely historically and academically. Because I am a herald, this same view of heraldry tends to persist throughout the Alphabet, chronicalizing current practice and ideas. Obviously, in a book such as this, there must be some degree of plagiarization; I can only hope that it is slight and critical rather than moronic.

As I have tried to make the book acceptable to the ever-increasing number of students, I have had to be selective. Too weighty a book would have defeated my object by forcing up the cost and confounding the neophyte with detail. In making my selection, I have omitted terms which have no special meaning in heraldry. Thus "fox" is not listed, although foxes are frequently found in arms, because the fox is depicted as in nature. On the other hand "fox's mask" is included as the word mask may well be foreign to those as unacquainted with the hunting field as they are with heraldic fields.

I have also omitted many obsolete, archaic and text-book terms which, if they were ever used, have long since been abandoned or forgotten. An occasional curious term has been included, because I thought it might be an old favourite with some readers, but such words have been stigmatized by an asterisk. Equally, I have not treated of the terminology of early blazon. This field has been admirably covered by Dr Gerard J. Brault in his recent book *Early Blazon*.

Orthography is always a problem, as no two armorists ever seem to agree as to how certain words, like fess (or fesse), or guardant (or gardant) should be spelled. In most cases I have used the spelling currently favoured in official blazon. The endings -é, or -ée I have anglicized to -y, except where the former endings still seem to be *de rigueur,* or where the word is a noun rather than an adjective. Paty, semy, bezanty have replaced paté, semé and bezanté as the principal spelling, but words like tenné, which is still usual, have remained. It has always seemed rather absurd that French adjectives, with their endings either masculine (semé) or feminine (semée) should be used to qualify English neuter nouns. The anglicization of such adjectival endings solves this problem.

When a herald writes a book on heraldry, he has the advantage of a certain amount of special knowledge. Unfortunately, this can also be a disadvantage inasmuch as some readers are bound to conclude that as the book has been written by a herald it must be regarded as *ex cathedra*. Such is not the case: if it were, *The General Armory* by Sir J. Bernard Burke, Ulster King of Arms, would be what some uninformed people believe it to be, the New Testament of heraldry. In fact, his critics dub it the Apocrypha of heraldry.

It must be remembered that armory is not an absolute science; on many points there can be two or more opinions and in a work of reference such as this, the author can only put forward his own views and be ready to stand by them, or be argued out of them.

I once knew a writer who was angry because a reviewer dubbed his work 'popular'. If any reviewer does me this courtesy, and if the public accepts his criticism, then he will have made three firm friends, my publisher, my agent and myself.

Heyford House
Oxfordshire

John Brooke-Little
Richmond Herald

August 1972

FOREWORD TO NEW AND REVISED EDITION

The request for a second edition within a year of publication is naturally very gratifying but, far more important, it has afforded me the opportunity of making some corrections and useful additions to the alphabet. I have also included a further ten illustrations drawn by Miss Alison Urwick.

I am grateful to those readers who have written making comments and suggestions; many of these have been implemented and I hope new readers will follow suit, in the pious hope that a third edition may be called for.

Heyford House
Oxfordshire

John Brooke-Little
Richmond Herald

April 1974

1

HERALDS AND THE BIRTH OF HERALDRY

Before what we call heraldry existed there were heralds. This fact is very often overlooked by those who study the art and science of heraldry. Most people would define heraldry as 'the study of coats of arms or armorial bearings' yet the systematic use of distinctive personal devices on shields is not found in England until the early thirteenth century, before which time Norman kings certainly had heralds at their courts. One of the principal duties of these officers, who were attached not only to the royal but also to great noble households, was to arrange the tournaments which were the aristocratic football matches of the Middle Ages. It was their task to declaim the prowess of those taking part in these mock battles and to act as referees. Heralds were also used as messengers in both peace and war, and it was only later, when the nobility started to use coats of arms, that they became experts in this particular science: indeed, they became so absorbed in it that eventually the study of coats of arms came to be known as heraldry. Although strictly speaking the word heraldry really encompasses all the activities of a herald, in the cause of simplicity I will here give it its narrower meaning.

If one looks at the Bayeux Tapestry, one will see that the warriors have various devices depicted on their shields and flags. These devices cannot be regarded as truly heraldic; for in the first place the same device is not used consistently by the same man; in the second place the designs do not seem to follow any particular form or order; and in the third place a study of the seals of the descendants of those who came over with the Conqueror indicates that any devices used were not hereditary.

Heraldry, as we know it, may be further defined as follows: it is an ordered system of personal and corporate symbolism following certain rules; it is hereditary in character; the bearing of arms is in the nature of an honour; and the principal vehicle for the display of arms is the shield.

Heraldry emerged some hundred or so years after the Norman Conquest of England in 1066. The lords and knights, who owed feudal service to the monarch, and therefore had to appear from time to time with their private armies, found it convenient to have a symbol by which they could easily be recognized. In the same way, these magnates needed to use a seal with which to authenticate their documents, for few people could read or write in the early Middle Ages. What could be more natural than to paint some bold and easily recognizable device on their shields, flags and on the coat armour which they wore over their mail and also to use the same device engraved on their seals? In this way they could always be readily recognized by a simple picture. (See illustration opposite page 20.)

The people who probably benefitted most from this new and colourful custom were the heralds, for their task of arranging tournaments must have been vastly simplified by this new and easy method of identification.

I would like here to interpose a fairy story which I think explains how the heralds probably came to have such a lively interest in coats of arms: an interest which later developed into a monopoly.

Once upon a time, it being customary to celebrate great occasions by holding a tournament, King John decided to hold one near London to celebrate the anniversary of his Coronation. He sent the royal heralds throughout the country to proclaim the news of this tournament and to invite the nobility to attend and take part. Right up on the Scottish border, in Cumberland, there lived a knight called Sir John. He was a simple fellow and not used to great occasions but he thought that it would make a holiday for his wife and family if he took them down to London for the tournament. So he raised a little money, gathered his family together, and set forth for the South. When he arrived at the tournament field he noticed that many of the nobility present were using coats of arms. (This expression, by the way, simply derived from the fact that the device was painted on the coat armour, as well as on the shield.) Now although Sir John had heard about coats of arms he had never actually considered using one himself, but seeing how attractive they looked, he approached one of his fellow knights, who had a rather splendid lion painted on his shield, and asked him about these coats of arms.

'Is there any reason,' he said, 'why I should not have a coat of arms?'

'None at all,' his acquaintance replied, 'you are a knight. You need to be recognized in the tournament, and presumably you need to use a seal from time to time. Obviously you are the sort of person who ought to have a coat of arms.'

Sir John was delighted with this news. 'Well,' he said, 'what I should like is a red shield with three golden lions on it.'

'Oh,' said his friend, 'you can't possibly have that; that is what the King uses and the whole point of coats of arms is that no two people shall use the same device. If I were you I would seek the advice of one of the royal heralds. If you cross his palm with silver I am sure that he will help you.'

Sir John was grateful for this advice and went off to find a royal herald. He soon discovered one and told him his troubles.

'Of course I shall be delighted to help you,' said the

herald, 'for I and the other heralds find it most helpful when arranging tournaments to have lists of who has what coat of arms. In this way we are able to advise people about what devices to use and so stop duplication. What had you in mind?'

'Well,' said Sir John, 'I have been told that I can't have three lions and I quite appreciate the reason why. I thought it might be appropriate if I had a red shield, as I'm rather keen on blood, and on it I would like three Scotsmen's heads, cut off at the neck and bleeding, because most of my spare time is spent lopping off the heads of marauding Scots.'

The herald obligingly made a rough painting of this coat, held it up and asked Sir John what he thought of it.

'As a matter of fact,' Sir John admitted, 'I really can't see the Scotsmen's heads at all. Their red hair, red beards and red faces just don't show up against the red shield.'

'Quite true,' said the herald, 'it is for this reason that I and my brother heralds have drawn up certain conventions, aimed at making arms as bold and distinctive, and consequently as useful, as possible. The principle convention is that coloured objects shall not be placed on a coloured shield. Therefore, if you have Scotsmen's heads with their ruddy complexions, you will want to put them on either a silver or gold shield. Naturally you will not be able to afford the precious metals themselves, and indeed they glitter so much and are so heavy that it is impractical to use them, but they are represented by white and yellow. Also as far as possible we use simple and conventional symbols, many of them of great antiquity, as these stand out better than pictorial representations and are therefore more clearly visible. Likewise we prefer to stick to bold primary colours as these show up more clearly than mixed colours and half tones.'

So Sir John settled on a silver shield with three red Scotsmen's heads on it. The herald said that as far as he knew no one had a shield too similar to this but he consulted one or two of his brother heralds to make assurance doubly sure. They consulted their books and rolls of arms but could find nothing too similar to the coat selected by Sir John. The herald therefore pronounced the new coat of arms unique and said that he and his brother heralds would make a note in their books that Sir John had adopted the arms in question.

Well, this is just a fairy story, but I feel sure there is more than a grain of truth in it, for we know that many of the early rolls of arms were compiled by heralds. It is also quite certain that by the end of the fourteenth century, when heraldry was firmly established, the royal heralds were asserting their armorial authority and the senior heralds (called kings of heralds of arms, or more simply just kings of arms) were making rules and regulations for the good order of coats of arms.

It is not difficult to see why heraldry became hereditary in character. As often as not a son would succeed his father in his land and it was therefore convenient for everyone if he used the coat of arms his father had before him. Younger sons were also wont to use their father's arms, being proud to bear them, but to distinguish themselves from the head of the family they made small alterations or additions to the arms. Nor is it difficult to see why arms were early regarded as ensigns of honour, for they were painted on the shield, which itself was considered an object of honour and respect. The profession of arms was an honourable and noble calling and a man's armour and weapons were regarded with veneration. Also it must be remembered that the only people who needed to use arms were the nobility: that is those who were worth recognizing in battle, who were invited to tournaments and who needed a seal. Arms, therefore, were regarded as ensigns of nobility or gentility and this is still true today.

Because arms were held to be an honour they were deemed to stem from the Crown, which is the fount of honour, and a measure of control was exercised by the sovereign to protect arms. When an armorial dispute arose it was settled in the Court of Chivalry, which was also known as the High Court Military or the Court of the Constable and Marshal. This court still exists and is today usually called the Earl Marshal's Court. It sits only rarely but it is a valid court of law and a distressed armiger (that is one who bears arms) may always have recourse to it if he feels aggrieved.

In the very early days of heraldry it is quite clear that it was nobles and knights who assumed arms, possibly with the help of the heralds. As time went on and the feudal system began to crumble, a middle class arose composed of people who were not of the greater nobility but who were rich and powerful. These sought to establish their gentility by obtaining a coat of arms and in the fifteenth century we find the kings of arms actually granting and assigning arms, on behalf of the Crown, to men who were not descended from the old nobility and who therefore had no hereditary right to arms. From the middle of the four-teenth century, corporations too started to use shields of arms both on their seals and to mark their personal property, and such bodies also sought regular grants of arms from the kings of arms.

It may seem strange that a corporate body, which neither wore armour, fought battles nor participated in tournaments, should want to use arms. But it must always be remembered that from the earliest days coats of arms were used not only in tournament and battle but also to beautify and identify. There are many tombs and brasses which are decorated with coats of arms. Also there are many early instances of armorial stained glass commem-orating a benefactor or a deceased person, and one has only to think of the famous Sion cope, made in about 1302, to appreciate that heraldry was also used to decorate textiles. It is therefore hardly surprising that corpor-ations should seek coats of arms for they were able to use them in much the same way as an individual. Indeed, the only way in which they could not use arms was in the tournament and on the battle field but in the fifteenth century the original and practical use of personal arms was already declining. Corporations were only too pleased to demonstrate that they were honourable bodies and to use and display insignia which enjoyed legal protection.

Let me now revert once more to the heralds, for the whole history of the development of heraldry is dependent upon the activities of these officers. As I have mentioned, not only the kings but also the greater nobles kept heralds. However, it is with the development of the royal heralds that I am principally concerned, for the employment of heralds by noblemen declined with the feudal system, whereas the importance and influence of the royal heralds increased as time went on.

By the reign of King Edward III, we have clear evidence that three ranks of herald existed and that it was customary to give heralds distinctive names or titles and to create them ceremonially with investiture and baptism.

The three ranks of herald are king of arms, herald and pursuivant. It is a little confusing that the word herald has become a generic term as well as being the name of the middle rank of herald. To avoid such confusion it is perhaps better to refer to heralds in general as officers of arms.

The kings of arms have territorial jurisdiction. Clarenceux King of Arms 'rules' south of the river Trent and Norroy King of Arms is king of the northern province. There is also a senior or principal king of arms called Garter King of Arms, an office created in 1415.

Various titles have been used for royal heralds, but for over four hundred years the titles used today have been consistently employed. The heralds are called Lancaster, Chester, Windsor, York, Somerset and Richmond. Their titles in most cases reflect the fact that their predecessors were originally private heralds who came into the royal service. Thus Richmond Herald was once private herald to the Earl of Richmond, but when Henry, Earl of Richmond, became King Henry VII he made his private herald into a royal herald and since then there has always been a Richmond Herald.

Originally the pursuivants were apprentices, but today their duties and responsibilities are much the same as those of the heralds. The pursuivants are Rouge Croix, Rouge Dragon, Portcullis and Bluemantle, which titles, as well as those of the heralds, are fully explained in the glossary.

Although the royal heralds had acted as a corporation within the royal household, under the chairmanship of Garter King of Arms, for much of the fifteenth century, they had no home of their own where they could keep their books and records. As their concern with coats of arms was now their principal activity, and presumably also a financially rewarding one, they wanted to have a common place of residence and a charter of incorporation giving them a legal, corporate identity. Such a charter was eventually granted them in 1484 by King Richard III and he also made over to them a house in the City of London. This corporation of the royal heralds is usually known as the College of Arms or Heralds' College.

The Charter of King Richard III is thought to have become null and void on his death in 1485; certainly the heralds lost their house in London, and it was not until 1555 that a new charter was granted them by King Philip and Queen Mary, who also gave them a freehold house in London. The present College of Arms building in Queen Victoria Street is situated on the same site, the old house having been burnt down in the Fire of London in 1666.

The heralds' duties today are much the same as they were in the fifteenth century. The kings of arms still grant arms and still make rules and regulations regarding matters heraldic. It is for this reason that the development of heraldry has largely depended upon the decisions and rulings of the kings of arms.

For example, one so often reads in manuals of heraldry that it is an unalterable rule that a colour cannot be placed upon a colour. Well, as I mentioned in my fairy story; for purely practical reasons this has long been a convention, but there is nothing to stop the kings of arms breaking this rule if they wish and there are in fact several examples of coats of arms which do not follow this particular canon.

The heralds are subject to the over-all jurisdiction of the Earl Marshal, an office which is hereditary in the family of the Duke of Norfolk. They assist him in arranging ceremonies such as coronations and state funerals and they also take part in these and other State occasions. As members of the Royal Household, they are still paid small salaries by the Crown. For example, that of pursuivant is £13.45 a year.

In addition they are allowed to keep the fees paid on grants of arms and are also permitted to act as professional consultants in heraldic and genealogical matters.

Although the kings of arms still grant arms with the royal authority, on receipt of a warrant from the Earl Marshal authorizing them to do so, it has long been customary for the other officers of arms to act as intermediaries between their clients and the kings of arms, designing arms and putting them before the kings of arms for their consideration.

People often ask whether arms are still granted today. The answer is very emphatically 'yes'. Arms are frequently granted to individuals and corporate bodies throughout the Commonwealth and honorary arms are granted to American citizens of British descent.

The ancient ceremonies which used to be observed upon the creation of a herald now no longer take place, the officers of arms being created by Letters Patent under the Great Seal. Although the Charter of 1555 limits the membership of the College of Arms to thirteen named officers, the Crown occasionally creates Heralds and Pursuivants Extraordinary, that is in contradistinction to the other heralds, who are Officers in Ordinary. Such appointments are made by Warrant under the Queen's Sign Manual and those appointed, although they take part in state ceremonies, are not members of the College of Arms.

One of the most significant parts of the ceremony of creating a herald was investing him with his tabard. The tabard or royal coat is a loose-fitting garment, with the royal arms of the reigning sovereign emblazoned throughout on the back, front and on each sleeve. The tabard has long been the distinctive dress of a herald and it is today worn by the officers of arms over their special household uniforms. (See illustration opposite page 21.)

2

THE DEVELOPMENT OF ARMS

Let us now consider the development of the coat of arms itself. At once one is bedevilled by ambiguous and loose terminology. People indifferently refer to *arms, a coat of arms, a crest* and *an achievement of arms*, in fact, each of these terms has a precise meaning which I will attempt to explain.

Illustrated opposite page 52 is an achievement of arms. This is a representation of all the armorial devices to which the bearer of arms is entitled.

Strictly speaking, the expression coat of arms, which is frequently shortened to arms, applies only to what is borne on the shield, but more often than not, the complete achievement is called a coat of arms and I think one must accept this common usage.

On the other hand, the word crest has a limited and definite use and should certainly never be used to describe the arms nor the whole achievement. The crest is simply the object modelled on top of the helm; in other words it crests the helmet. The creatures shown on either side of the arms form part of the complete achievement and, with a logic and simplicity rarely found in heraldic terminology, are called supporters. Beneath the shield is a motto which, curiously, is not an integral part of the coat of arms. In England mottoes are never now included in the wording of a grant of arms; thus it is possible for two or more people to use the same motto and they may change their motto when they wish. This is not true in Scotland where mottoes are included in the actual grant of arms.

Around the shield is the motto of an Order of Knighthood and beneath the shield depend various decorations. These are the personal insignia of the bearer of the arms and are not hereditary armorial devices.

Let us now examine the component parts of the shield in detail. The most important part of any achievement of arms is the shield, for it is on this that the principal hereditary devices are borne. Before anyone thought of using a crest on a helmet, the bearing of arms on a shield was well established.

On the second great seal of King Richard I, struck in about 1195, he is depicted on horseback in full armour. On his shield are the three lions, which are the arms of England and on his helmet a lion is painted on the fan crest. This is an early example of a form of crest, but it was not for some hundred years after the death of Richard that crests came to be used and regarded as an additional hereditary device. Helms, which previously had had fans or plumes of feathers on them, now came to be decorated with objects modelled in the round and affixed to the top.

For the same reason that arms assumed an hereditary character so also did crests, and when a person showed his full armorial bearings he depicted the shield and placed above it the crest, together with the helm onto which it was fixed. Even those who never actually used a crested helm, which must have been a cumbersome object, adopted a crest for use in pictorial representations of their achievement.

Round the base of the crest is usually shown a coronet, cap, or wreath of twisted scarves, which probably originated in the favours that ladies bestowed upon the knights of their choice before a tournament. The knights would take the scarves and bind them round the base of their crest.

Also attached to the helmet was a short mantle or cloak, which probably had the dual effect of deflecting both a sword blow aimed at the neck and also the fierce rays of the sun on the back of the metal helm.

Sometimes in representations of arms the helmet, with its mantling, is omitted and the crest on its wreath is placed above the shield. There is nothing technically wrong with such a representation, but it is to some extent a solecism when one considers the origin of the crest.

Likewise, the crest and wreath is often used on its own, or in conjunction with the motto, to mark small objects of property, such as spoons, rings and so forth. In these instances, the engraver has usually no idea what a crest and wreath really are, and so shows the wreath as a pole or bar rather than two strands of soft material woven together.

It is sad but true that in the eighteenth and nineteenth centuries the heralds were relatively inactive and hid their light under a bushel. It is particularly sad when one remembers that these centuries were periods of great industrial advancement and many humble families achieved wealth and distinction, either in the industrial world, or through colonial expansion. Naturally, like the Tudor merchants before them, such people sought the insignia of gentility – a coat of arms. However, being unaware of the existence of the heralds, who for their part took no pains to make themselves known, these people often went to stationers, silver smiths or unofficial 'heraldic offices' to ask whether they could discover their arms or crest so that they could put them on their writing paper, silver and so forth. These tradesmen, not wishing to loose a commission, were only too ready to discover or invent arms or crest, or else accord to their clients the arms of another family having the same name, but otherwise unconnected. In this way, literally thousands of spurious, or wrongly attributed arms and crests came into existence. It is only since the great revival of interest in heraldry, which has taken place since the last war, that many of these spurious coats have come to light, often having been used for some two hundred years or even longer. Unfortunately, whilst this revival of interest has led to much legitimate heraldic activity; it has also encouraged unprincipled tradesmen to offer an uncritical and often snobbish public a variety of goods, evilly emblazoned with a coat of arms used, probably without any authority, by a person having the same surname.

The fact that arms are granted to an individual, and to the legitimate descendants of his body in the male line, cannot be too strongly stressed. In fact, arms descend in much the same way as a surname, but only from the grantee, not from his brothers, uncles or cousins unless such relatives were specifically included in the terms of the grant of arms. Thus it is that all the male descendants of the grantee bear the arms, with small marks of difference to distinguish them one from the other, and daughters of the family bear arms in a way which I shall discuss later, until such time as they marry.

Supporters are of more recent origin than crests. Isolated instances of creatures supporting arms are found in the early fifteenth century, but at this date they cannot properly be considered as part of the hereditary armorial bearings. They were probably first used as an artistic device by seal engravers who, in order to fill the gap between the shield and the circumference of the seal, intruded creatures, often based on badges used by the owner of the seal. These were later used in other representations of the arms and so, in the sixteenth century, the heralds came to have cognisance of supporters, recognizing them as armorial ensigns and making rules for their use. Today, supporters are only granted to peers of the realm, Knights of the Garter, Thistle and St Patrick, to Knights Grand Cross and Knights Grand Commander of the Orders of Chivalry and to certain corporations, more or less on an *ad hoc* basis. Sometimes the supporters are shown standing on a grassy mound or an ornamental bracket. Such a resting place, called a compartment, does not usually form part of the grant of arms and it can be altered or omitted at will. The supporters to the arms of life peers and knights are personal to the grantee and are not hereditary. Those of peers are inherited with the peerage.

Insignia of orders of knighthood can be shown in an achievement of arms if this is so desired and the various orders have regulations embodied in their statutes detailing how such insignia may be used. In the same way decorations, such as the Military Cross or the Territorial Decoration, may be suspended beneath the shield but campaign medals ar not so used.

Peers of the realm may place their coronet of rank above their shield and certain personal insignia, such as the baton of a Field Marshal, may also be used in the ways prescribed.

In the illustration it will be seen that the mantling is spattered with a badge. This is quite distinct from the arms. Originally the great medieval paladins used badges with which to mark their retainers and also small articles of property. These badges were usually associated more with a manor or honour, than with the person himself. The knot of the Staffords and the ragged staff of the Warwicks are well-known examples of medieval badges.

After the end of the feudal period, badges were not much used and were certainly not granted by the kings of arms. Where a badge was needed, such as on livery buttons, the crest was generally employed. However, at the beginning of the present century the Earl Marshal authorized the kings of arms to grant badges to anyone who was already entitled to arms.

Although today the use of badges by individuals is not widespread it is certainly increasing and a great many corporate bodies find it convenient to be granted a badge, for they still have retainers or their modern equivalent, and own property which can more suitably be marked with a simple badge than with the complex and more dignified achievement of arms.

Civic and municipal authorities find badges of great

value, for they frequently receive requests from local bodies, not themselves eligible for a grant of arms, to use the arms of the corporation. Now no armiger may license another to use his arms. To do so would be to trespass on the rights of the kings of arms, who alone may grant arms. On the other hand, refusal can lead to ill-feeling. What then can a corporation do? The answer is, that it may licence the use of its badge. In this way, the Law of Arms is observed and honour is satisfied.

I have mentioned that women bear arms differently from men. This is because the vehicles for displaying arms and crests are part of a man's armour, namely the shield and helm: because of this bellicose connotation they are not considered suitable for a woman. A maiden lady bears the arms of her father, without difference or distinction, upon a diamond-shaped figure called a lozenge and as she has no helm she cannot exhibit a crest. When she marries her husband's arms are united with hers, either by impalement, or if she is an heraldic heiress, by placing her arms on a small shield, called an escutcheon of pretence, in the centre of his. This then becomes the marital coat. If she is left a widow she must revert to the use of a lozenge containing the marital arms.

An heraldic heiress is a woman whose father left no living male issue, nor children of dead sons at his decease. Thus, if a man dies leaving four daughters, these four daughters are all regarded as co-heirs of their father and are treated as heraldic heiresses. This means that when they marry they place their arms in a shield of pretence over those of their husband and on their death their children inherit their arms as a quartering.

The word quartering is confusing, for it immediately suggests a division into four quarters. This was obviously its original meaning in heraldry, referring to a shield divided into four so as to accommodate more than one coat of arms. However, as heraldry became more complicated, it was often necessary to represent more than four coats of arms on one shield and so shields came to be divided into six, eight or more portions, each one containing a coat of arms inherited from an heiress and each, illogically, being called a quartering. The diagram opposite page 53 illustrates more clearly than any words how the quarterings are inherited and displayed.

A quartered shield is read from left to right like a book. The first coat is the patronymical coat, the next is the first quartering acquired, in the third quarter is the second quartering acquired and so forth. If, in the cause of symmetry, there is a blank at the end of the shield, then the patronymical coat is repeated. When there is only one quartering, then it is of course necessary to repeat both quarterings, in the manner shown in the diagram.

Apart from women, the only other classes of armiger who use a special display of arms are county councils and ecclesiastics. A county council may be granted a mural crown to ensign its shield in place of a helm and crest; an Anglican bishop uses a mitre in place of a crest and Roman Catholic clergymen and dignitaries use a variety of distinctive ecclesiastical hats over their shields of arms. For some reason unknown to me, Anglican clergy beneath the rank of bishop still bear arms with crest and helm, but once episcopal dignity has been attained these are discarded in favour of the mitre.

3

THE GRAMMAR OF HERALDRY

I have already inferred that no rules of heraldry are so sacrosanct that they cannot be set aside by the kings of arms, whose authority is virtually absolute. On the other hand, I must point out that such conventions as exist are there for very good reasons and they are only ever set aside in exceptional circumstances.

It is therefore possible to rationalize the science of heraldry and to detail the conventions which, by and large, have been employed by heralds throughout the centuries.

Before considering what goes on a shield, let us examine the herald's paint box. In the first place, he has two metals at his disposal, gold and silver. Although gold leaf or gold paint is sometimes used, the two metals are most frequently represented by yellow and white. The heraldic words for the metals are taken from the French and are *or* (gold) and *argent* (silver). Then there are five colours: *gules* (red), *azure* (blue), *sable* (black), *vert* (green) and *purpure* (purple). The last two, not being primary colours, were used but seldom in medieval heraldry, but have increased in popularity with the growth of paper heraldry. There is also a number of 'stains' which are occasionally employed, but which in my opinion should be avoided whenever possible, as they are so easily confused either with each other or with certain colours. They are *tenné* (orange), *murrey* (the purple-red of the mulberry) and *sanguine* (a deep blood-red).

An object may also be shown in its natural colours, in which case it is termed *proper*. Finally, there are various furs, namely: *ermine*, *erminois*, *ermines*, *pean* and *vair* and refinements of *vair*. These are all described in detail in the glossary.

The general convention is that a metal shall not lie on a metal, nor a colour on a colour. The furs are technically considered to be neutral; that is, you may put either a colour or a metal on a fur and vice versa. In fact, if you put a silver lion on an ermine shield it is not going to show up and such a coat would consequently be regarded as bad heraldry, although it would be technically correct. It is very doubtful if a king of arms would allow such a coat to be granted, in spite of the fact that it fulfils the letter of the law. In all the rules of heraldry it is the spirit rather than the letter of the law which should be followed.

It must here be remarked that heraldry has a terminology of its own. There are some who consider this to be tortuous jargon, but my own experience has shown that, generally speaking, people enjoy using the ancient words, mostly drawn from the old Norman French which would have been the everyday language of the early heralds. I have found no real desire among armorists to describe armorial insignia in the vernacular.

When one considers an achievement of arms one always places oneself behind it as if actually carrying the shield and wearing the helm, so that the left-hand side of the shield as you look at it becomes the right or *dexter* side. Likewise the right-hand side is the left, or *sinister* side. The background is termed the *field* and anything placed on the field is a *charge*; thus a shield with three lions on it is said to be charged with three lions, each lion being a separate charge. The top portion of the shield is called the *chief* and the bottom the *base*. For convenience, most heraldic writers have classified the various types of charge. The plain geometrical charges, such as the *chevron*, the *bend*, the *fess*, the *pale*, the *cross* and the *saltire* are called *ordinaries*. Lesser geometrical charges, such as *cantons* and *piles*, are termed *sub-ordinaries*, whilst other charges are grouped under such natural classifications as beasts, monsters, birds, fishes, reptiles, insects, flora and inanimate objects; these, again, are obviously capable of sub-classification. With the possible exception of the *ordinaries* which are accorded a certain precedence, there is no particular magic in these classifications. If an *ordinary* is repeated on a shield, then it must be drawn more narrowly than usual; this makes it a *diminutive* of the *ordinary* and it is given another name. One does not have three *fesses* on a shield, but three *bars*; two *bendlets* rather than two *bends* and so forth. The field of a shield may either be plain, scattered with charges (*semy*), divided in the direction of an ordinary, such as *per chevron* or *per fess*, or divided by repeating the diminutive of an ordinary, in which case it is termed *bendy, paly, barry*, or whatever, *of so many pieces*. What is true of the shield is also true of the charges on it. Thus, you can have a *lion semy of crosses, an eagle bendy of six pieces or and azure,* or a *grenade per pale argent and sable.*

The lines used in heraldry do not have to be straight and there are many variations which can be used, either in drawing ordinaries, their diminutives, or lines dividing the shield. Common variations on the straight lines are *engrailed, invected, embattled, wavy, nebuly* and *indented,* but there are many others which will be found in the glossary.

In the earliest days of heraldry few beasts were used and by far the most important of these was the lion, who was generally found in one of two positions, standing upright and waving all his legs in the air, termed *rampant*, or walking along, called *passant*. Later, more and more beasts were introduced into heraldry and more and more stylized positions were contrived for them. The heraldic menagerie soon filled up with *boars, bears, stags, horses, talbots* and a host of other creatures. They were found sitting (*sejant*), walking (*passant*), rearing up (*salient*), lying down (*couchant*) and so forth.

Sir Geoffrey Luttrell (after the illumination in the fourteenth century Luttrell Psalter). His arms are displayed everywhere, even on the dresses worn by his wife and daughter-in-law who hold his crested helm and shield.

If the beasts look out of the shield and not to the dexter, as all things normally do in heraldry, then they are termed *guardant* and, if looking over the shoulder, *reguardant*. Of birds, the most common and noble is the eagle, usually shown *displayed,* that is, spread out as if forcefully flung at a wall. After the eagle the *martlet* is probably found most often. This little bird, depicted without any feet, was probably originally a swift, whose feet are scarcely visible. Doves, Cornish choughs and pelicans are also popular.

The dolphin and the lucy (an old name for a pike) head the aquatic section, the *dolphin* usually being shown either upright (*hauriant*) or swimming along (*naiant*).

Heraldry is full of intriguing monsters, chief among which are the *griffin*, the *unicorn* and the *dragon*. Not surprisingly, reptiles are not very popular, although *serpents* tied in a knot (*nowed*) occur quite often and one entwined about a rod forming the *Rod of Aesculapius* appears in the arms of many doctors and medical institutions.

The bee is by far the most popular insect, being a symbol of industry and is usually depicted *volant*, that is with wings outspread as in flight.

The rose (the common five-petalled dog-rose) is the king of the heraldic garden, but it is quite surpirsing what a variety of flowers, fruit, leaves and trees have been used in coats of arms.

When one comes to inanimate objects, then almost anything goes, but certain ancient, conventional objects still retain their popularity. For example, a soldier generally prefers to have a *sword* or a *grenade* to symbolize his military prowess than to sport a representation of the latest tank; the sun as a symbol of light and energy is usually preferred to an electric light bulb; and a man called Miller is still more likely to use the ancient mill rind to pun on his name than a representation of an actual miller. Nevertheless, heraldry contains such diverse objects as a *DNA double helix* (granted in 1966) and a *distillatory double armed with two worms and bolt receivers* (granted in 1639). Fortunately the use of such outlandish curiosities is the exception, not the rule.

To describe arms in heraldic language is to *blazon* them. *Blazon* is a sort of shorthand based on a series of conventions, which enables a person to draw arms accurately from a description. Blazon should be brief, unequivocal and euphonious. Probably the best way to learn how to blazon is to obtain a copy of an old reference book such as a Peerage or Baronetage containing illustrations and blazons of arms, and work through these to see how the blazons are arrived at. Here I propose only to state a few of the basic conventions which are followed when blazoning arms. In the first place the colour of the field is described, next the charges on it are detailed, adjectives other than quantitative following the nouns they qualify, the name of the tincture coming last. Thus, the blazon of a red shield containing three silver rampant lions would be: *gules* (the colour of the field) *three lions rampant* (the position of their bodies) *argent* (their tincture). No further description is necessary, for the following conventions apply:

1. Where three like charges are placed on a shield, two are always deemed to be in the chief and one in the base unless it is mentioned otherwise.
2. The term rampant has a specific meaning and so need not be described further.
3. When lions are either red themselves, or are placed on a red shield, their tongues and claws are always blue; so it would not be necessary to mention this unless they were of a different colour.

If the three lions were in a row in the middle of the shield and if their tongues and claws were green, then the shield would have to be blazoned: *gules three lions rampant in fess* (that is following the direction of a fess and not in the conventional two and one position) *argent, armed and langued* (special terms used when referring to the claws and tongue) *vert*.

If there is an ordinary on the shield, then this is generally considered more important than the other charges and is mentioned first, with the exception of the chief and the *bordure* (see glossary). If the first coat mentioned above contained a gold chevron charged with three blue crescents it would be blazoned: *gules, on a chevron or, between three lions rampant argent, as many crescents azure*. Here the convention is followed that if three charges are placed on a chevron they will be placed one in the middle and one on either side, upright and not following the direction of the chevron. The use of the expression *as many* is only a nicety of blazon and is introduced simply to avoid the tautology of repeating the word three; it is not essential, but it can be euphonious.

It is outside the scope of this brief introductory essay to list all the conventions of blazon. Indeed, it would not be possible to do so. They can easily be found in the textbooks devoted to heraldic grammar. I hope, however, that I have indicated the way in which a herald's mind works when blazoning a coat of arms.

When blazoning a full achievement, after the arms have been described, the crest is blazoned. Most crests proceed from a wreath, yet the blazon of a crest containing a wreath begins *on a wreath of the colours* (the colours being deemed to be the principal metal and colour in the arms). In fact, of course, this only lends credence to the idea that the crest sits on the wreath, whereas the wreath should surround the crest. I submit that it would be far more sensible if the blazon of a crest began, *within a wreath of the colours* or even *out of a wreath of the colours*.

There was a time when the wreath, of which six twists are usually shown, invariably consisted of the colours. Recently, however, there has been a reversion to earlier practice and the wreath may now be of any metals and colours desired. This also applies to the mantling which, in the seventeenth century and earlier, was always red outside and silver inside; later it followed the colours of the wreath but now the outside may be of any colour or colours and the inside of one or both of the metals. This again is a reversion to earlier practice and, from an artistic point of view, gives the designer of arms much greater scope. After describing the wreath the crest is then blazoned in the ordinary way.

As actual crests have not been used for many hundreds of years, some quite impossible charges have been granted as crests, but in this field also there is a conscious movement to return to earlier principles and design crests which are at least capable of being modelled in the round. Unfortunately, it is not always possible to do this successfully, as it is often difficult to discover a crest which is unique and at the same time aesthetically pleasing.

Another problem with the crest is that there are rules governing the position of the helmet. These rules were devised at the beginning of the seventeenth century and might have been intended to play into the hands of those who think only in terms of paper heraldry and are not prepared to consider the possibility of the crest being three-dimensional. These rules are as follows: the helmet of a corporation, an esquire or gentleman, is of steel with closed visor and faces the dexter; that of a knight or a baronet has the visor open and faces the front; that of a peer is of silver with five gold bars facing half towards the dexter and the royal helm is all of gold, barred and faces the front.

The royal crest is a *lion statant guardant* which, when placed on the royal helm, is shown sideways on to the helm. If it were actually modelled on to the helm it would be facing out towards you but then it would have to be blazoned differently. Let us take as another example a *lion sejant* granted to a man for his crest. This looks very well as it naturally faces the dexter which is the direction of the helm and it could well have been worn in a tournament.

But what if this same man is created a knight? His helmet has to face the front but the lion crest must remain facing the dexter, for if he turned with the helm, he would at once become a *lion sejant affronty*, which might well be somebody else's crest. Unfortunately, for this very reason, it is too late to put the clock back. All that can be done to obviate the absurdity which arises when the crest faces one way and the helm another is to twist each slightly towards the other, although not so much that the blazon of the crest would have to be altered.

Finally, if the arms contain supporters, these are blazoned. If they are identical, then the blazon will start *on either side . . .* , but if they are dissimilar then the dexter supporter is blazoned first.

4

THE LAW OF ARMS

By the law of arms I mean the actual laws which govern the way in which arms are inherited and in which they may be used. The rules or conventions of heraldry are sometimes termed the laws of arms but this only leads to confusion. They are regulations promulgated by the kings of arms, some of which might well be upheld in the Court of Chivalry, but they constitute the lore rather than the laws of heraldry.

The first thing to understand about the Law of Arms is that it is not common law but civil law, and the Court of Chivalry is a civil court. In England the ecclesiastical courts, the Court of Admiralty and the Court of Chivalry were the only courts where the Roman civil law was administered. The lawyers who practised in these courts were not the ordinary common lawyers but civilian proctors and advocates. On the other hand the civil law is not some sort of ancient Roman wizardry; it is as much part of the law of England as laws enacted by Parliament. It is the procedure which pertains in the Court of Chivalry and other civil courts, which differs from that used, for example, in the Court of Queen's Bench.

Mr George Squibb, QC, Norfolk Herald of Arms Extraordinary and himself learned in the civil as well as the common law, summed the matter up in *The Law of Arms in England* (revised edition 1967) when he wrote:

> It is impossible properly to appreciate the surviving records [of the Court of Chivalry] unless it is firmly borne in mind that the law administered in

the Court of Chivalry was a branch of English Law, albeit not the Common Law, and that recourse was only had to the Civil Law when the answer was not to be found in the customs and usages of the Court. To know the law of arms in England we must seek the customs and usages of the Court of Chivalry as interpreted by the civil lawyers.

What then are the customs and usages referred to? Many have emerged from the reports of cases heard before the Court, others have yet to be put to the test, but it is possible to make certain basic propositions with the fairly sure knowledge that if ever these were challenged before the Court they would be upheld.

The first is that arms may not be assumed at will but must be the subject of a lawful grant of arms made by a competent authority. Arms are in the nature of an honour rather than a piece of personal property. If the latter were the case then the common law which governs the inheritance of property would have to take cognizance of arms. This it does not do. As the Crown is the fount of all honour arms must stem from the Crown just as they are protected by the Crown in the Court of Chivalry. This particular facet of the Royal Prerogative has for many centuries been exercised by the kings of arms, although since 1568 the prior consent of the Earl Marshal has to be obtained before the kings may exercise the power vested in them by the Crown. In practice this regulation was not observed until about a century later, but thereafter the first step that a prospective grantee of arms must always take is to petition the Earl Marshal for his Warrant to the kings of arms allowing them to grant.

The second proposition is that once arms have been granted they may be borne and used by the grantee, as his especial, personal mark of honour and likewise by his legitimate descendants in the male line, as described earlier in this essay. They may be used by none other than one who is entitled to them by grant or descent. This does not mean that they may not be displayed by another. To display arms is simply to exhibit them in a way which clearly indicates that they are the arms of someone else. For example many people display the arms of towns on pieces of commemorative porcelain and the like; they exhibit the arms of schools, colleges and institutions with which they have some connection; and frequently the arms of famous people are used as decoration. All this is permissible and indeed to be encouraged. On the other hand to use a seal ring engraved with another's arms or to place on stationery arms to which no title has been proved constitutes a bearing and using of arms, and is wrong: that is, it is not only pretentions and vulgar but is legally indefensible. Whilst an armiger can do what he likes with his arms, good taste being his only guide, he may not allow another to use them, for, as has been noted, by doing this he would be usurping the powers of the kings of arms who alone may grant arms. Anyone who wishes to circumvent the normal laws of inheritance and let someone bear his arms who has no right to them by descent, must seek a Royal Licence to effect this. For example a bastard or adopted child has no right to bear his father's or adoptive father's arms except under the terms of a Royal Licence. Such licences are directed to the Earl Marshal and must be recorded in the College of Arms before becoming effective.

The third and last proposition concerns the nature of arms. As has been seen arms are ensigns of honour rather than articles of property. They are frequently and correctly referred to as *tesserae gentilitatis*, the insignia of gentility. A grant of arms is not a bestowal of nobility; it does not, like Letters Patent creating a peerage, ennoble the recipient. It simply acknowledges the gentility, either innate or acquired, of the grantee. In the old days, when grants of arms were couched in more flowery language than they are today, and with long preambles, they frequently set forth exactly what arms were and why a particular grant was being made. The preamble to several grants made by

John Smart, Garter King of Arms, 1450-1478, may be paraphrased thus:

> Equity requires and reason ordains that the merits of virtuous, noble and courageous men shall be regarded by fame and that not only they but also the issue of their bodies shall be seen to be pre-eminent above others by the display of certain signs [that is, arms, helms and crest] of honour and gentility. In this way they shall give an example to others to spend their days in feats of arms and virtuous works with a view to making their own lives renowned and gentle. Also, I, Garter King of Arms, am advised by the report and testimony of other noble and reliable men, that John Smith has long pursued feats of arms, borne himself valiantly and conducted himself honourably so as to deserve well and that he and his posterity may be accounted well worthy to be numbered among the company of other ancient, gentle and noble men. Now as a remembrance of this his gentility I have devised, ordained and assigned to him and his heirs arms, helmet and crest, in manner following . . .

and here the arms are blazoned.

This or a similar form of words was common in the fifteenth and sixteenth centuries and makes the nature of a grant of arms very clear. It is a recognition, by the bestowal of hereditary symbols, of an existing and persisting status. To read more than this into a grant of arms would be foolish, but it would be equally incautious to denigrate a grant of arms to the status of a private document. It is, and unless the law is altered, will remain a solemn, public, legal document, recorded in the proper registry for such deeds, the College of Arms and protected by the law of England.

5

THE ALPHABET

Aaron's Rod   (see **Aesculapius, Rod of**)

Abaised   (also **Abased or Abaissé**) Occasionally used to describe a charge which is borne lower than its usual position.

Abatement   A mark of dishonour added to arms. It exists in literature but not in fact, except in Scotland. Recently the so-called guilty party in a divorce action matriculated arms and was assigned a gusset sanguine as an abatement for adultery. (See **Gusset, Gore, Delf** and **Point**)

Abbot   An abbot may ensign his arms either with a plain white mitre (*mitra simplex*) or with a black ecclesiastical hat having three tassels pendent on either side. He may also place a crozier behind his shield either in bend or in pale. An Abbot Nullius Dioceseos uses the same insignia as a Bishop. (See **Bishop**)

Abisme*   (also **Abyss**) Term used to describe a minor charge in the centre of the shield but drawn smaller than usual.

Abouté   Placed end to end.

Accollé   Two shields placed side by side and touching; also occasionally used as a synonym for gorged or entwined about the neck.

Accompanied   (also **Accompagné**) Sometimes used in blazon in place of 'between'; i.e. 'a chevron between three bezants' can be blazoned 'a chevron accompanied by three bezants'.

Accosted*   Side by side.

Accrued*   A tree which is full grown.

Achievement The complete armorial bearings. Used in contradistinction to its various parts – arms, crest, supporters, motto, etc. (See Introduction, page 11)

Addorsed (also **Adossé, Endorsed** and **Indorsed**) Placed back to back; frequently used of the wings of birds when shown in such a position.

Adumbration Used of a charge which is of the same tincture as the field, being shown as a shadow or in outline. Baynton of Yorkshire (1565 *Visitation*) bore: 'or, on a fess between three crescents gules, a lion adumbrated' (or *en umbre*). This word also refers to the shading used when simulating relief in the depiction of charges.

Adopted children These may be granted the arms of their adoptive parents but a Royal Licence must be sought and the arms when granted are differenced by the addition of two links of a chain interlaced, either fesswise or palewise.

Distinction
for adopted
children

Adoption, Arms of (See **Arms of adoption**)

Aesculapius, Rod of A serpent entwined about a rod. These were the attributes of the Greek god Aslepius (Latin: Aesculapius) of medicine; hence this charge is frequently used in the arms of doctors and medical institutions. It is sometimes called 'Aaron's rod'.

Rod of
Aesculapius

Affronty (also **Affronté**) Facing the observer. The crest of Scotland is a lion affronty.

Lion sejant
affronty

Agnus Dei (See **Paschal Lamb**)

Aiguisé* Pointed. 'Urdy' is the term normally employed.

Air Force Cross (See **Distinguished Flying Cross**)

Aislé Winged.

Aland (also **Alan, Alant** and **Alaunt**). A large hunting dog with short ears.

À la Quise (See **Quise, à la**)

Alisé Rounded. Used of the ends of the traverses of certain crosses.

Allerion (also **Alerion**). An eagle displayed but without beak or legs. It occurs in the arms of Lorraine.

Alliance, Arms of (see **Arms of alliance**)

Alphyn A monster of unsettled form. It is sometimes shown with tufts and claws like the heraldic tyger, but in Fenn's *Badges* its fore-legs are ox-like, with cloven hooves, and it is less hirsute than in other representations. It is noted as being a badge or beast of the Lords de la Warr.

Alphyn

Altar Usually shown rectangular, but sometimes circular. It is nearly always enflamed.

Ambulant* Walking.

Amethyst Used for purpure when blazoning by jewels. (See **Jewels**)

Amphiptère* A winged serpent.

Amphisbaena Usually described as a serpent with a head at either end of its body but in the crest of Gwilt (granted 1728) the amphisbaenae are shown as the lizards which they properly are.

Amphisbaenae
as in the
crest of Gwilt

Amphisien cockatrice (See **Basilisk**)

Anchor Normally shown upright and with a ring at the top. When a rope is attached and entwined about the shank or beam it is called a 'foul' anchor or an anchor 'cabled'. The cross-piece is termed the 'stock' or 'timber'; the barbs are called 'flukes'.

Anchored (also **Ancré** and **Anchory**) Used to describe a cross whose traverses end in the flukes of an anchor.

Ancient (also **Auncient** and **Anshient**) Possibly a synonym for a standard but more usually applied to a small flag ending in a point. An 'ancient crown' is a form of crest coronet with a treflated design. It was first so blazoned in the grant of arms to The Heraldry Society in 1956. (See **Crown**). A coronet composed of four fleurs-de-lis rising from a rim is sometimes called an 'ancient coronet'.

Ancient user A claim to bear arms by ancient usage is so called. Jurists argue that such usage must date back to 'time immemorial', which under the common law is held to be 1189, but it may be further argued that in the Court of Chivalry the Norman Conquest was regarded as the limit of legal memory. In the seventeenth century it was generally agreed that if a person could prove a prescriptive usage from the beginning of the reign of Queen Elizabeth I ancient user could be presumed.

Angle A piece of metal, generally L-shaped and with rings at each end, used for strengthening a fabric, but also applied to any angled figure.

Animé (See **Incensed**)

Annelled Ringed; e.g. a bull with a ring through its nose is sometimes blazoned 'annelled'.

Annodated* Embowed in the form of the letter S.

Annulet A ring. It is the mark of difference used for a fifth son. Two annulets interlaced are sometimes called a 'gimmel ring'. A pattern of interlaced annulets is termed 'a network of annulets interlaced'.

Annuletty (also **Annulated** and **Annuly**) The ends terminating in rings.

Antelope (also **Argasill**) The heraldic antelope, as opposed to the natural creature, is shown with an heraldic tyger's face, tusks, serrated horns, an antelope's body, tufts down the spine and a lion's tail. The heraldic antelope is usually now so blazoned to avoid confusion with the zoological beast.

Heraldic
antelope statant

Apparent Used when something is apparent or visible. The crest of a family of London of Bedfordshire consists of a tower with a man issuing from the top and is blazoned 'apparent'.

Apaumé (also **Apaumy, Appaumé** and **Appalmed**) Of a hand or gauntlet when open with the palm showing.

Apres (also **Apre** and **Apree**) A monster having the body of a bull and tail of a bear. One is a supporter to the arms of the Merchants of Muscovia (Muscovy Merchants).

Apres

Aquilated* Semy of eagles' heads.

Arblast (also **Arbalest**) Synonym for a cross-bow. One is borne by a family of Arblaster.

Archbishop The Archbishops of York and Canterbury sit as peers of Parliament and have precedence over dukes. They and other Anglican Archbishops bear arms in the same way as Anglican bishops (see **Bishop**) but sometimes substitute a single traversed cross for a crozier. A Roman Catholic Archbishop either ensigns his arms with a jewelled mitre (*mitre pretiosa*) or with a green ecclesiastical hat having ten tassels pendent on either side. He may also place a double traversed cross in pale behind his shield.

Arch This may be either single, supported by two pillars, or double, supported by three. The type of arch should be detailed in the blazon.

Arched (also **Enarched** and **Archy**) Bent in the form of an arch; frequently used in connection with a chief, fess or chevron. If two curves are shown the term 'double arched' or 'double enarched' is used. (See **Partition, Lines of**)

Chief arched

Archiepiscopal Cross   (See **Episcopal Staff**)

Argasill*   (See **Antelope**)

Argent   The metal silver. It is usually represented by white, as silver tarnishes. In engraving the surface is left plain. It is variously abbreviated *a.*, *ar.*, or *arg.*

Crest of a
sinister
arm embowed

Arm   The human arm is either found 'embowed', 'bent' (cut off at the shoulder and flexed at the elbow) or 'cubit' (cut off below the elbow). When an arm embowed is shown in armour it is sometimes, though rarely today, termed an 'arm vambraced'. The blazon should always note whether the arm is dexter or sinister.

Crest of a
dexter
cubit arm

Armed   Used to describe the offensive and defensive portions of a creature's anatomy when of a different tincture from that of the body. It comprehends horns, claws, talons, beaks and tusks but does not preclude the use of more specific terms, such as 'beaked' and 'horned', if these are preferred. When used of humans, or parts of the human body, it means encased in armour. It can also refer to the heads of arrows, but the term 'barbed' is more usual.

Armes parlantes (See **Canting arms**)

Armiger One who bears arms.

Armigerous Entitled to bear arms.

Armilliary sphere (See **Celestial sphere**)

Arming buckle (See **Buckle**)

Armorial bearings Synonym for an achievement of arms.

Armory The correct word to describe the study of armorial insignia. The expression 'heraldry' has superseded it in popular parlance, but strictly speaking the term heraldry encompasses all the duties of a herald, not merely that occupation for which he is most noted (see Introduction, Chapter 1). An Armory is a dictionary of arms listed under surnames. The most noted printed Armories are Edmondson's, Berry's, Robson's and Burke's.

Armour Unless specified in the blazon armour may be either plate or mail, although the latter is more frequently found.

Arms This term is often freely used when referring to the complete achievement, but really should be applied only to the actual shield and what is borne upon it.

Arms of adoption Arms assumed by someone not entitled to them by descent. Today this can be done only in pursuance of a Royal Licence. The most usual reason for such assumptions is to comply with an injunction in a will, which requires the beneficiary to take the name and arms of the testator in order to inherit.

Arms of alliance An expression used to describe arms where more than one coat is shown on a shield so as to illustrate the alliance of families through marriage.

Arms of assumption In medieval times the victor in a combat occasionally assumed the arms of his victim. Such cases are rare but the arms so taken are sometimes called 'arms of assumption'. They should not be confused with 'assumed arms', which are arms borne without lawful authority.

Arms of community A dated expression for what are more usually styled 'corporate' or 'impersonal' arms; that is, the arms of a corporate body rather than those of an individual.

Arms of concession Arms conceded by one person to another as a reward. (See **Augmentation**)

Arms of descent Inherited arms, in contra-distinction to arms acquired by grant.

Arms of dominion These, which are also styled 'arms of sovereignty', are those borne by a sovereign in respect of the territories he rules rather than his own family arms. The royal arms are arms of dominion; the Queen's arms of descent would be those of her branch of the House of Saxony. Arms of dominion do not follow the ordinary rules and conventions of armory but are settled *ad hoc* by the monarch, usually, of course, with ministerial and heraldic advice.

Arms of office Arms borne in respect of holding a certain office, such as those of the kings of arms. These may be borne impaled with the personal arms of the holder of the office. Such arms are also referred to as 'official arms'.

Arms of pretension Arms borne to illustrate a claim to territories not actually possessed, such as the use of the royal arms of France by the kings of Great Britain until as late as 1801.

Arms of sovereignty (See **Arms of dominion**)

Arraswise* Used to describe a square charge with one of its angles facing the observer.

Arrondie* (also **Arrondi** and **Arondi**) Rounded or curved.

Arrow Arrows are frequently used as charges, either singly or tied in bundles or sheaves. The position of the arrow should always be noted in the blazon. Frequently the points and feathers of the arrows are of a different tincture from the shaft. In such cases the arrows are usually described as 'barbed' and 'flighted', but the expressions 'armed' and 'feathered' are occasionally employed.

Ascendant* Rising upwards.

Aspectant* (See **Respectant**)

Aspersed* (See **Semy**)

Assumption, Arms of (See **Arms of assumption**)

Assurgent Rising out of; usually applied to creatures rising from the sea.

Astral crown A coronet composed of four pairs of wings, each enclosing a mullet of six points, set upon a rim. It was designed during the last war to symbolize pre-eminence in aviation. (See **Crown**)

At gaze Term used to describe beasts of the deer species when standing and facing the observer. It is synonymous with 'statant guardant'.

Atomic heraldry As might be expected, various representations of symbols connected with nuclear physics have been used in heraldry in recent years. One, blazoned 'the conventional representation of an atom' was granted to the Society of Electronic and Radio Technicians Ltd. Other representations, variously blazoned, are to be found in the arms of Warwick University and Sir Ian Orr-Ewing, whilst in Lord Penney's arms are two symbols of the paramagnetic electron in the third and one of it in the second harmonic.

Attainder A 'Bill of Attainder' was a legal process which had the effect of corrupting the blood of the accused. The goods, titles and arms of an attainted person could not be inherited by his heirs until such time as the attainder was reversed by Act of Parliament.

Attired Word used to describe the antlers or attires of beasts of the deer variety. It is also occasionally used to describe the clothes of a human being, but the terms 'vested' and 'habited' are more usual.

Attires   (See **Attired**)

Attributed arms   Arms which are invented for someone who never bore them. The medieval heralds attributed arms to pre-heraldic monarchs, saints and biblical characters. Ancient rolls of arms sometimes begin with a series of these fanciful coats. Thus the Fitzwilliam version of the Heralds' Roll (*c*. 1270-80) begins with the arms of Prester John, the Emperors of Rome and Constantinople, and St Edward the Confessor, and Bowyer's Book (*c*. 1440) starts with the arms of Brutus, Albanactus, Camber and Belinus. Arms are still invented for saints and the attributes of Christ in connection with the dedication of churches. There are, for instance, many coats of arms attributed to St Paul, St John, the Precious Blood, the Passion of Christ, the Assumption of the Blessed Virgin and so forth.

Augmentation   A mark added to an existing coat of arms to commemorate some notable achievement. There are two types of augmentation, those granted in pursuance of a Royal Warrant and those granted by the kings of arms at the instance of the armiger himself. Royal augmentations, or 'augmentations of honour', were freely granted after the restoration of Charles II, during the Napoleonic Wars and throughout the nineteenth century. They usually take the form of a chief, canton or inescutcheon and often also of an extra crest, borne to the dexter of the family crest.

Aulned*   (also **Awned**) Used of barley when bearded.

Avellane   (See **Cross**)

Averdant*   Covered with herbage.

Aversant*   Clenched; the antonym of apaumé.

Azure   The colour blue. It is usually represented by a bright blue such as cobalt. In engraving, horizontal lines are used to indicate azure. It is abbreviated *b*. *Az*. is sometimes found but most armorists avoid it as it can be confused with *ar*. (argent).

Badge A device which is not part of the coat of arms but which armigers use on standards, to mark retainers and to identify small articles of personal property. A person may have more than one badge, different badges being used in respect of different properties or enterprises. After the end of the feudal period badges were not much used but their use was revived in 1906, when an Earl Marshal's Warrant empowered the kings of arms to grant badges to armigers, whether persons or corporations. There is some uncertainty as to the way in which badges devolve and to the extent to which an armiger may license or allow another to use his badge. However, it is probably true to say that where arms are inherited as a quartering, so is the badge appertaining to those arms. Equally, it can be argued that a person may allow another to use his badge as long as by doing so the rights of the kings of arms are not infringed.

Bagwyn A monster resembling the heraldic antelope with the tail of a horse and long curved horns. It was once a supporter of the arms of the Fitzalan Earls of Arundel.

Bagwyn

Balance A pair of scales. Both terms have been applied indifferently for both the standard variety and that which is held in the hand. However, in recent grants the term 'balance' has been used solely for the former type and 'pair of scales' for the latter.

Banded Tied round with a band. Frequently used of garbs and sheaves of arrows when banded of a different tincture from the charge itself.

Banner A square or oblong flag emblazoned throughout with the arms. The greater nobles, down to the rank of knights banneret, were entitled to banners of varying proportions, although it is unlikely that the dimensions laid down were actually adhered to. Today banners intended for outside use tend to be longer than they are deep. A fair-weather flag has the proportions three to two. Ceremonial banners, such as those of the Knights of the Garter at St George's Chapel, Windsor, are still square.

Bannerole (also **Banderolle**) A small banner used at funerals to display the arms of families allied to the deceased.

Bar An ordinary which, like the fess, traverses the centre of the shield horizontally. It differs from the fess inasmuch as it is narrower and several may be borne on the shield. Textbooks often state that it cannot be borne singly but this is not so as there are several examples of a single bar.

Bar gemel Two narrow bars close together i.e. twin (Latin — *gemellus*) bars: rather like train lines. A bar gemel is seldom, if ever, borne singly. In fact, in early blazon the two bars were simply called 'a gemel'.

Bar between two bars gemels

Barbed This refers to the sepals of the heraldic rose which appear between the petals; to the human beard; to the point of an arrow; and sometimes to that of a spear. If an arrowhead has two barbs, one above the other, it is termed 'double barbed'.

Barded* (See **Caparisoned**)

Barnacle An instrument used by farriers to curb a horse when breaking it. It is usually referred to as a 'pair of barnacles' or as a 'brey' or 'horse brey'. It can be borne closed (as by Wyatt of Kent) or extended (as by Geneville).

Barnacle

Baron The fifth and lowest rank in the peerage. Originally great feudal lords beneath the rank of earl were called barons but from the thirteenth century the style was reserved for those who received writs to attend Parliament. Later still barons were created by patent. By the Appellate Jurisdiction Acts of 1876 and 1887, the Crown was empowered to create Lords of Appeal in Ordinary barons for life. By the Life Peerages Act 1958 the Crown was further empowered to create anyone a peer for life. (See **Peer** and **Coronet**)

Baroness The title of the wife of a baron or that of a woman who holds a barony in her own right. Baronesses in their own right usually use the title 'Baroness', whilst barons' wives generally prefer the style 'Lady'.

Baronet An hereditary title, between that of knight and baron, introduced by King James I in 1611 to raise money for the plantation of Ulster. Baronets are entitled to use a knight's helmet; that is, full-face with the visor raised. Baronets of England and Ireland (created between 1611 and 1707), of Great Britain (created between 1707 and 1801), and of the United Kingdom may augment their arms with either a canton or an inescutcheon argent charged with a sinister hand, couped at the wrist gules. Baronets of Scotland or Nova Scotia were created between 1625 and 1707 for the plantation of Nova Scotia. They suspend their neck badge beneath their arms from an orange-tawny ribbon. In 1929 King George V assigned a neck badge for use by all baronets other than Scottish. It may also be suspended beneath the arms.

Baronet's
shield of
augmentation

Badge of
baronets of
Nova Scotia

Barrulet   A diminutive of the bar. The term is now rarely used, the word 'bar' doing service instead.

Barry   (also **Barruly**) Divided barwise into an even number of divisions. The actual number is sometimes specified, sometimes not.

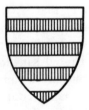

Barry of eight

Barry-bendy   Divided barry and also bendy.

Barry-bendy

Barry-pily A field divided into an even number of pieces by piles placed barwise.

Barry-pily

Barwise Charges arranged horizontally, following the direction of the bar. The term 'fesswise' is used in the same context.

Bar sinister A popular misnomer for the 'baton' or 'bendlet sinister', which are used as marks of bastardy. 'Barre' in French heraldry is the bend or bendlet sinister of English heraldry — hence the confusion.

Base (also **Point**) A division, corresponding to a chief but at the bottom of the shield; also the area at the foot of the shield. (See **Points of the Shield**)

Basilisk A monster which resembles the cockatrice but usually has a dragon-like head on the end of its tail; for this reason it is sometimes called the 'amphisian cockatrice' (See **Amphisbaena**). That the two monsters were often confused is demonstrated in the blazon of the supporters of Lord Curzon of Penn. They are basilisks but are called cockatrices with tails terminating in dragons' heads.

Basilisk

Bastardy A bastard child has neither name nor arms, but he may petition for a Royal Licence to be granted the arms of his father, if paternity is acknowledged or can be proved, with a suitable mark of distinction. The usual mark of bastardy since the late eighteenth century has been the bordure wavy, but the bendlet sinister was once frequently used. Bordures plain, compony and engrailed are also occasionally found. The baton sinister has been used almost exclusively for royal bastards. The arms of William IV's nine bastards, the Fitz Clarences, were differenced by a variety of batons sinister.

Bordure wavy

Bendlet sinister

Bath, Order of the The Most Honourable Order of the Bath has its roots in the Middle Ages. It was revived in 1725 and it has subsequently been enlarged and its statutes altered on various occasions. Today there are two divisions, military and civil, and three classes, 1 Knight Grand Cross, 2 Knight Commander and 3 Companion. All classes suspend the appropriate insignia beneath their arms and encircle their shields with the motto. Holders of the first class are entitled to a grant of supporters and may place the collar of the order round their arms. The order has its own king of arms and its chapel is in Westminster Abbey.

Baton   (also **Baston**) A bendlet couped at either end. It is usually found borne sinister (i.e. from sinister chief to dexter base) as a mark of bastardy, particularly in the arms of royal bastards. A baton is also the insignia of office of the Earl Marshal and of a field marshal and two batons of appropriate design are placed in saltire behind the arms of these dignitaries.

Battering ram   A cylindrical shaft, banded and with rings for suspension. At one end is a ram's head.

Battering ram

Battle axe   Usually shown with an ornamental shaft and a point at the back of the blade.

Battle axe

Battled   (See **Embattled**)

Battlement, Piece of   A strip of embattled wall looking exactly like a mural crown (see **Crown**) is sometimes blazoned a 'piece of battlement'.

Beacon   An open bucket of fire on a pole with a ladder, usually shown on the sinister side.

Beacon

Beaked Used to describe the beaks of birds and monsters.

Beam (See **Shank**)

Bear arms To be armigerous. One is only entitled to bear and use one's own lawful armorial insignia; but one may display any coat — that is, exhibit it — so long as it is not in such a way that it would seem to be one's own. Thus it is not wrong to display arms of schools, boroughs or even famous families; it is offensive only to bear and use a coat, as it might be on stationery and personal jewelry, which is not one's own.

Bearing Another rather archaic word for a charge. Bearings Armorial is a flowery way of referring to an achievement or complete coat of arms.

Becket (also **Beckit**) This would seem to be a colloquial word for the chough. The attributed arms of St Thomas Becket are: argent three choughs proper.

Bee A popular symbol of industriousness. It is normally shown displayed as if pinned to a specimen board but is blazoned volant.

Bee volant

Beehive Normally the domed hive is portrayed. It is usually 'beset with bees'.

Beetle* This word for the maul or mallet is to be found used in the name of public houses called 'The Beetle and Wedge', but it is not common in heraldry.

Bell The type of bell should be specified in the blazon as both church and hawk's bells are fairly common charges. If a blazon simply refers to a bell, then it is usually safe to assume that it is a church bell.

Belled Having a bell or bells appropriately attached; i.e. round the neck of a cow, on the points of a jester's cap, etc.

Bend An ordinary consisting of a broad band extending from dexter chief to sinister base. Charges on a bend follow the direction of the bend unless otherwise specified. When charges are placed on a shield in the direction taken by a bend they are said to be 'in bend'.

Bend

Bendlet The diminutive of the bend. It is normally about half the width of the ordinary but the eye, not the ruler, is the guide of the true armorist, just as it is of the artist.

Bend sinister A bend reversed, that is, running from sinister chief to dexter base. The bendlet can likewise be borne sinister. It is the bendlet sinister not the bend sinister which has frequently been used as a mark of bastardy.

Bendwise Lying in the direction of the bend.

Bendy A shield divided bendwise into an even number of divisions. If the lines go from sinister chief to dexter base then it is termed 'bendy sinister'.

Bendy of six

Benediction   A hand 'raised in benediction' is a hand apaumé with the first and second fingers erect, the others being closed.

Beset   (See **Beehive**)

Bezant   (also **Besant** and **Besaunt**)   Term applied to a roundel when it is gold. As bezants were originally gold coins most textbooks state that they should not be shaded to show relief but they sometimes are and I doubt whether any great crime is committed. The term 'talent' means a bezant but is seldom, if ever, used.

Bezanty   (also **Bezanté**)   Semy of bezants.

Bicapitated*   Having two heads.

Bicorporate   Having two bodies.

Big   A provincial term for wheat or possibly barley. Two ears of big occur in the canting arms of Bigland.

Bill   (also **Forest bill, Bill hook** and **Wood bill**) An implement with a curved blade used for lopping trees. The blade is found borne without the haft.

Billet   An oblong rectangle like a train ticket.

Billety   (also **Billeté**)   Semy of billets.

Billety

Bird bolt   A short, blunt arrow used for shooting birds. The ends of bird bolts vary in design, some being flat, some round, whilst others are forked.

Bird bolt

Bishop The twenty-four bishops of the Established Church who sit as peers of Parliament rank between barons and viscounts. All Anglican bishops surmount their arms. with a mitre in place of a helm, mantling and crest. Sometimes a crozier is placed in bend or in pale, or two croziers are displayed in saltire behind the shield, but this affectation, though probably unexceptionable, is not now fashionable. Diocesan bishops may impale their personal arms with those of their see, the latter being shown on the dexter side. Roman Catholic bishops may ensign their personal arms either with a jewelled mitre (*mitra pretiosa*) or with a green ecclesiastical hat having six tassels pendent on either side and may place either a crozier in bend or in pale, or a single traversed cross in pale behind their shield. When Anthony Watson, Bishop of Chichester, was granted arms in 1596 the shield was ensigned by a black bonnet rather than a mitre, with its suggestions of popery.

Blackamoor's
head

Blackamoor A Negro. The usual charge is a black-amoor's head, which is also sometimes called a Negro's head. It is frequently confused with a moor's head, which strictly speaking should have Arabic rather than Negroid features.

Blasted (also **Blighted** and **Starved**) A tree which is leafless and withered.

Blazon To blazon arms is to describe them in correct armorial terminology so that they can be correctly rendered from the verbal description, which is itself called a blazon. Although there are certain definite conventions as to how arms shall be blazoned (see Introduction, page

22) many of the supposedly hard and fast rules laid down in heraldic manuals are often ignored. For example, tautology was once a mortal sin. A tincture or number was never repeated in a blazon; the person blazoning the arms had to have recourse to such devices as 'of the third', meaning of the third tincture mentioned. The result, though not tautologous, was tortuous in the extreme. In grants of arms today the kings of arms favour a more literary style of blazon, repeating tinctures and numbers if it is euphonious to do so and sometimes using the terms gold and silver for or and argent, as did the medieval heralds. Official blazons are unpunctuated and tinctures and the names of charges begin with a capital letter.

Blemished Used of a charge, such as a sword, which is broken.*

Bleu céleste A pale sky-blue. This tincture, new to English armory, has been used in several recently granted coats of arms where the grantee has some connection with aviation.

Blighted (See **Blasted**)

Bluebottle This is the cornflower, not the insect.

Bluemantle Pursuivant The title of one of the four pursuivants in ordinary. Its use dates from the early fifteenth century and it almost certainly refers to the blue mantle of the Order of the Garter. The badge is a blue mantle, lined with ermine and having gold tassels.

Boar The wild boar is portrayed with a large head, exaggerated tasks and a fan of bristles down the back. A boar's head is a common charge. It is either couped or erased behind the ears or at the neck. The former method is favoured in Scotland and the latter, but by no means to the exclusion of the former, in England.

Boar

THE MARSHALLING OF ARMS

Henry Owen = Jane, heir of John Green

Marital coat

James Iles = Lucy, co-heir, with her sister   Janet, co-heir with her sister

Marital coat

Herbert Iles = Mary, hr. of Robert Smith   Gloria Iles   Mark Olds

Benedict Iles   Patric Olds

Diagram showing how arms are marshalled on marriage and
how quarterings are inherited.

Body heart (See **Heart**)

Bonacon (also **Bonasus**) A bull-like monster but with horns which curl inwards, a short mane and a horse's tail. Its horns being useless, it defends itself by shooting its burning excrements at its enemies. It appears to have been first granted to Richard Chandelor in 1560, as a crest.

Crest of
Chandelor

Bone Unless a particular bone is specified the heraldic bone is one with a knob at either end.

Bonnet Although this term is sometimes applied to the crimson cap turned up with ermine which is shown within a peer's coronet, it is the electoral bonnet that is best known in British heraldry. This bonnet surmounted the inescutcheon of the arms of Hanover in the royal arms from 1801 until Hanover was declared a kingdom in 1816.

Book An increasingly popular charge, especially in the arms of universities, colleges and other places of learning. The blazon should indicate whether it is open or closed and also whether it has clasps or seals attached.

Bordure A border running round and up to the edge of the shield. In an impaled coat the bordure is not continued down the palar line. A bordure wavy has been the usual mark of bastardy (q.v.) in England since the late eighteenth century. In Scotland the bordure compony is used for the same purpose.

Boreyne A monster not unlike a Bonacon (q.v.) but it has a tongue like a spear-head, a dorsal fin, the fore-legs of a lion and hind-legs terminating in eagle's claws.

Boreyne

Boteroll (See **Crampet**)
Bottony (See **Cross**)
Bouget (See **Water-bouget**)
Bourchier knot (See **Knot**)
Bourdon (See **Palmer's staff**)
Bourdonné (See **Cross**)

Bow The long bow is meant. It is usually shown bent; but if it is unbent this should be mentioned. If the string is of a different tincture from the bow the term 'stringed' is used.

Bowen knot (See **Knot**)

Braced Interlaced, especially of chevrons, as in the arms of Fitz-Hugh.

Branch It is sometimes difficult to distinguish between a branch and a sprig (q.v.) but the former would obviously be larger and bear more foliage.

Bretessed Used of an ordinary which is embattled and counter-embattled, the inward and outward embattlements lying opposite each other. Lord Llewelyn-Davies bears a fess bretessed, as does a family of Mann granted arms in 1814, but at that time the expression was not used and the fess is simply blazoned 'embattled counter-embattled'.

Fess bretessed

Brey   (See **Barnacle**)

Bridge   There is no stylized form of bridge in heraldry although the charge is not uncommon. The type of bridge (i.e. number of arches, form of crown, etc.) should be carefully blazoned. For example, Lethbridge, baronet, bears a bridge of five arches, embattled and with a turret over the centre arch.

British Empire, Order of the   The Most Excellent Order of the British Empire was instituted in 1917 and has subsequently been extended and altered. There is a military and civil division and five classes, 1 Knight Grand Cross, 2 Knight Commander, 3 Commander, 4 Officer and 5 Member. All classes suspend the appropriate insignia beneath their arms and the first three classes encircle their arms with the circle and motto. Holders of the first class are entitled to a grant of supporters and may place the collar of the order round their arms. The order has its own king of arms and its chapel is in the crypt of St Paul's Cathedral.

Brisure   (also **Brizure**)   Mark of Cadency.

Broad arrowhead   A pheon or arrowhead but with the inside edge of the point unserrated. This distinction between the pheon and broad arrow is not always observed in blazon.

Brock   A badger. It is the canting crest of several families of Brooke. It is also known as a grey, but this term is rarely, if ever, used.

Buck   (See **Stag**)

Buckle   Round, oval, square and lozenge-shaped (arming) buckles are frequently found. In blazon it is safest to detail the type of buckle, the way it lies on the shield (if not upright) and the position of the tongue.

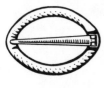

Oval buckle   Square buckle   Arming buckle

Bugle horn (also **Hunting horn or Horn**) A simple curved horn. The bands round the horn are known as virols or bands and it is frequently shown stringed, the string being tied in a bow above the horn. It seems to be a matter of caprice as to whether the horn faces the dexter or sinister but current practice is for the mouth to face dexter.

Bugle horn

Bullet* A roundel sable.

Burgeonee When a fleur-de-lis is shown with petals closed in the form of a bud about to open it is so described. This expression was first coined after the Second World War.

Cable   The rope attached to an anchor.

Caboshed   (also **Cabossed**) Applied to an animal's head when shown affronty but cut off clean behind the ears so that no part of the neck is visible. The term is not applied to the heads of lions or leopards; for those the word 'face' is used.

Stag's head
caboshed

Cadency   The medieval tenet 'one man one coat' made it necessary for every cadet of a family to difference his arms from those of the head. This is called cadency. At one time clear differences such as a change of charge or tincture were usual but since the end of the fifteenth century small charges have been added to the shield. (See **Difference, Marks of**). In Scotland an elaborate system of bordures is normally used.

Caduceus   The rod of Mercury or Hermes. It consists of a rod about which two serpents are entwined, having at the end two wings surmounted by a petasus ball, pine cone or similar object. A symbol of speed and prudence; not to be confused with Aesculapius' rod.

Caduceus

Calopus   (See **Chatloup**)

Caltrap   (also **Galtrap** and **Cheval-trap**) A pointed iron implement. They were strewn on the ground to spike horses' hooves and so impede them.

Caltrap

Calvary (See **Cross**)

Calygreyhound A rare monster. It has the head of a wild cat, frond-like horns, tufted body and tail, rather like a lion's, and fore-limbs which end in claws. It was a badge of the Vere family.

Calygreyhound

Camel The one-humped variety is usually depicted but the Bactrian or common camel with two humps has also been used, as in the arms of Cammell of Derbyshire. No distinction is made in blazoning the two varieties.

Camelopard The giraffe, once thought to be a hybrid twixt camel and pard. John Bossewell, writing in 1572, describes it as being powdered with the spots of a pard, having a head like a camel's, the neck of a horse and feet like those of a young bull. Certainly there are some curious representations of this beast to be found.

Camelopardel* A giraffe with two long horns curving backwards.

Canadian pale (See **Pale**)

Cannon The muzzle-loading variety is shown unless otherwise indicated.

Canon A canon of a Roman Catholic Cathedral

Chapter ensigns his arms with a black ecclesiastical hat having three tassels pendent on either side.

Canting arms (also **Allusive arms** and **Armes parlantes**) Arms which pun or play on the name of the bearer. For example, Haseley of Suffolk bore a fess between three hazel nuts, and Cokerell a cross between four cocks.

Canton A square portion of the shield, smaller than the quarter, in the dexter chief. Augmentations are frequently granted on cantons. If a canton is shown in sinister chief it is blazoned 'a sinister canton'.

Canton

Cantoned* Said of a cross placed between four charges.

Cap-à-pie (also **Equipped**) A man armed from top to toe in complete armour is said to be 'armed cap-à-pie' or, rarely, 'equipped'.

Cap Various articles of headgear are so blazoned. (See **Chapeau**)

Caparisoned Applied to a horse when bridled, saddled and armoured. The terms 'equipped' and 'barded' are occasionally found in this context. (See **Cap-à-pie**)

Carbuncle (See **Escarbuncle**)

Cardinal Above his arms a cardinal places a scarlet ecclesiastical hat having cords with fifteen tassels interlaced with gold thread pendent on either side. He may also use such other insignia as may be appropriate to his degree.

Carnation (also **Charnel** or **Charnois**) Flesh-coloured. This term, much used in Tudor blazon, is sometimes still employed.

Carpenter's square (See **Square**)

Cartouche Scroll ornament round a shield. Often found decorating the oval figure on which continental ecclesiastics are wont to display their arms; thus it is often applied, though not strictly correctly, to such an oval.

Castle Two crenellated towers joined by a like wall in which is a port, although it is current practice to blazon this 'a port with two towers'. When a third tower is shown above the gate it is termed a castle triple-towered. Other varieties of castle should be blazoned as shown. Sometimes a single tower is, confusingly, blazoned 'a castle'.

Castle
triple-towered

Castor A beaver. That granted as a crest to William Patricke in 1561 is so blazoned.

Cat-a-mountain (also **Musion**) The wild cat. The domestic cat is simply blazoned a cat unless of a definite species, like the Siamese cats which support the arms of Lord Snow.

Catherine wheel (also **Katherine wheel**) A wheel usually having eight spokes, each one ending in a curved spike. It represents the intended instrument of martyrdom of the recently discredited St Catherine of Alexandria.

Catherine wheel

Cavendish knot (See **Knot**)

Celestial crown A crown of eight high points (five of

which are seen), each terminating in a small star, usually a six pointed mullet. (See **Crown**)

Celestial sphere (also **Armilliary sphere**) Normally depicted on a stand of indeterminate size. It is sometimes called an 'armilliary sphere' and sometimes, as in the arms of the Clockmakers' Company, simply a 'sphere'.

Celtic Cross By a decision of the kings of arms made in 1956 two varieties of cross are blazoned as 'a celtic cross'. These are as illustrated.

Two types of Celtic Cross

Centaur A creature from Greek mythology having the body and legs of a horse but with a man's trunk, arms and head. Usually found holding a bow and arrow and then termed a 'sagittary' or 'sagitterius'.

Chain Unless specifically blazoned a chain may be drawn with oval, round or square links, the first being the most usual.

Chape (See **Crampet**)

Chapeau (also **Cap of maintenance** and **Cap of estate**) The heraldic representation of this cap, once worn by the greater nobles, is of red velvet with an ermine rim ending in two points. It sometimes occurs as a charge but was principally used in place of a wreath or coronet on the helm. Today it is granted only to peers. In Scotland it is also granted to feudal barons actually in possession of the barony. Feudal barons who are not in possession but are representers have azure chapeaux.

Chapeau

Chaplet (also **Garland**) A circular wreath of leaves with four flowers in cross. Unless the blazon specifies the genus of flower the heraldic rose is shown.

Chaplet

Charge Anything borne on the shield or on another charge. Writers have classified charges, calling the important geometrical charges 'ordinaries' and the less important 'sub-ordinaries'. Others have been grouped into beasts, birds, monsters, fishes, reptiles, etc. Pedants frown on these arbitrary distinctions but they are now almost universally used and as many students find them helpful they would seem to be justified. Anything which has a charge on it is said to be 'charged'.

Charger This refers to a dish or platter, not to a horse.

Charnel or Charnois (See **Carnation**)

Chatloup (also **Calypus** and **Calopus**) A monster with a wolf's body, cat's face and goat's horns. It occurs as the crest of Sir Godfrey Foljambe and in the arms and crest granted to Thomas Cathorne in 1553, where it is blazoned 'proper' and shown as white with brown spots.

Chatloup

Chequy (also **Checky** or **Checquy**) Term applied to a field or charge divided into small squares of two alternate tinctures.

Fess chequy

Cherub A child's head between two wings. The plural 'cherubim' is sometimes used.

Chess rook (also **Cocke** or **Zule**) This is not a representation of the actual piece but is usually shown as having a bifurcated top.

Chess rook

Chester Herald The title of one of the six heralds in ordinary. Originally a herald attached to the princely appanage of Chester but since 1525 a herald in ordinary. His badge is a garb ensigned by the royal crown.

Cheval-trap (See **Caltrap**)

Chevron An ordinary issuing from the base of the shield shaped like an inverted V. If it depends from the chief it is termed a 'chevron reversed'. The chequers on a chevron checky or compony follow the direction of the chevron.

Chevron

Chevronel The diminutive of the chevron.

Chevronny　Divided into an even number of divisions chevronwise.

Chevronwise　In the direction of a chevron.

Chief　An ordinary which consists of the top part (usually about a third) of the shield. Some armorists hold that the chief is a division of the field, others that it is a charge placed on the field. Those who follow the latter theory are probably right, as coloured chiefs are seldom, if ever, placed on coloured fields and the same is true of metal chiefs on metal fields. A charge in the top portion of the shield is said to be 'in chief'. (See **Points of the shield**)

Chief

Chrystal　Sometimes used for argent when blazoning by jewels but 'pearl' is more common. (See **Jewels**)

Cinquefoil　A figure having five petals or leaves. If it has a hole in the centre it is termed 'pierced' of whatever tincture shows through the hole.

Cinquefoil

Circle of glory　(See **Glory**)

Civic crown　A wreath of oak leaves and acorns.

Clarenceux King of Arms　The senior of the two English provincial kings of arms. His jurisdiction lies south of the River Trent. Clarenceux has had the southern province since 1420. His official arms are: argent, a cross gules, on a chief of the last a lion passant guardant crowned or.

Clarion (also **Claricord, Sufflue, Clarendon, Organ rest** or **Rest**) Thought by some to have been a lance'or spear rest, but it was almost certainly a musical instrument. It is now invariably blazoned 'clarion'.

Clarion

Cleché (See **Cross**)

Climant* Means salient when applied to a goat.

Close Refers to a bird with its wings folded, or a helmet with its visor closed.

Closet A diminutive of the bar. The term is rarely used.

Clouds These are always billowy clouds. A bordure of clouds (as in the arms of the Royal Overseas League) is usually drawn as what might be called a 'bordure nebuly cotton-woolly'. There are examples of such a bordure simply being blazoned 'nebuly' but this is confusing as the two bordures are drawn differently.

Coat armour A coat of arms. A 'man of coat armour' is an armiger.

Coat of arms Originally this meant just the arms which were borne on the coat armour worn over the armour itself. Today it is commonly used to refer to the full achievement of arms.

Cock This refers to the common farmyard or dunghill fowl. If any other sort of cock is intended, such as heath-cock or moor-cock, it is so blazoned.

Cockatrice A monster which is like a wyvern but has a cock's head and barbed tongue. (See **Basilisk**)

Cockatrice

Cocke (See **Chess rook**)

Coded Used to describe the scrotum of an animal (usually a boar) when of a different tincture from the body. (See **Sexed**)

Cognizance A badge.

Cog wheel The variety usually shown is a wheel with an embattled edge and a single small hole in the centre.

Coker A high shoe. This charge occurs in the canting arms of Coker of Dorset.

Coheir (also **Coheiress**) (See **Heir**)

Collar There are various collars used in heraldry but the unqualified word refers to a plain circlet. The collars of the orders of chivalry as worn on collar days may encircle the arms of certain degrees of knight (see the various orders). The collar of SS is worn by serjeants at arms, heralds, kings of arms and certain other officers and it may encircle their arms. It is composed of linked esses and has a royal badge pendent.

Collared Having a plain collar round the neck. A simplification of the blazon 'gorged with a plain collar'.

Collar gemel A collar composed of two pairs of narrow bars. (See **Bar gemel**)

College of Arms (also **Heralds' College**) The familiar name for the Corporation of the Kings, Heralds and Pursuivants of Arms. Although the royal officers of arms acted as a corporate body from the early fifteenth century they did not receive a charter until 1483/4. The thirteen officers of arms in ordinary were reincorporated by King Philip and Queen Mary in 1555 and were given Derby House just below St Paul's as a residence. The present

College, built after the Great Fire of 1666, stands on the site of Derby House with its entrance in Queen Victoria Street. The official records are kept at the College, and from 10 a.m. to 4 p.m. from Monday to Friday one of the officers, known as the Officer-in-Waiting, is always on duty to answer questions and give advice. Fees are charged if professional work is undertaken. The College is owned and governed by a Chapter, composed of the three kings, six heralds and four pursuivants of arms, which meets monthly. Garter King of Arms presides over Chapter and the Earl Marshal has what, in the cause of simplicity, may be described as visitorial powers. (See Introduction, page 7)

Colours The 'colours' in a coat of arms are the principal metal and colour in the coat; 'a wreath of the colours' is a wreath composed of these. The actual colours used in heraldry are red (gules), blue (azure), black (sable), green (vert) and purple (purpure). Orange (tenné), mulberry colour (murrey) and blood-red (sanguine) are also occasionally used but are generally termed 'stains'.

Columbine Usually shown pendent from a stem curved to the dexter.

Columns If the blazon does not detail the type of column or pillar then it is usually best to show a simple Norman or Early English one, but frequently the style of architecture will be indicated.

Comb The crest of a cock. If this is of a different tincture from the body he is usually termed 'combed' although 'crested' is also used. If the ordinary hair-comb is depicted the variety with teeth on both sides is invariably shown, as in the arms of Ponsonby, Earls of Bessborough.

Combattant Used of two beast when rampant face to face. Sometimes they are termed 'rampant combattant', but this is unnecessary as the latter term embraces the former.

Comet Shown as a star with a trail of light behind it.

Community, Arms of (See **Arms of community**)

Companions of Honour This order, which confers neither title nor precedence and has but one class, was instituted in 1917. Members may suspend the insignia of the order beneath their arms.

Compartment The base, be it a scroll, grassy mound, waves of the sea or whatever, on which the supporters rest. If it is not part of the official blazon it may be omitted or altered at will, but if it is actually granted it must always be shown as blazoned. Today compartments, unless granted, are not usually depicted on grants of arms.

Compasses These are usually shown as what are now called dividers, expanded and with a point at the end of each limb, rather than with a pen or pencil at one end. In the original grant of arms to the Carpenters' Company of London, made in 1466, the compasses contained in the arms are simply blazoned 'iii Compas', rather than three 'pairs of compasses', as they would be today.

Complement (also **Plenitude**) A moon 'in her complement' is a full moon.

Compony (also **Componé, Gobony, Goboné** and **Gobonated**) A charge which is composed of a single row of equal divisions of two alternate tinctures is so described. If there are two rows, then the term 'counter-compony' or 'compony-counter-compony' is used. If more than two rows then it is chequy.

Bordure compony
and
fess compony-counter-compony

Concession, Arms of (See **Arms of concession**)

Coney Term usually used to describe the common rabbit.

Conjoined Joined together. 'Three lozenges conjoined' means three lozenges just touching each other. Two wings 'conjoined in lure', as in the arms of Seymour, means that the wings are joined at their bases, with tips downwards in the form of a falconer's lure.

Contourné (also **Tourné**) Signifying that the whole charge has been reversed to face the sinister.

Corbie A raven. It is blazoned in this way in the arms of Corbet of Shropshire so as to pun on the name.

Corded Tied with a cord; often a synonym for banded.

Cordelière (also **Cordon**) A knotted silver cord which encircles the arms of widows. It is occasionally found on hatchments but it is a rare conceit in England. In Scotland a widow whose paternal family is not armigerous may bear her late husband's arms in a lozenge within a cordelière.

Cornish chough This bird, a rare though once common member of the crow family, is nearly always blazoned 'proper' and is shown black with red legs and bill, which should be thinner and more curved than that of other crows. (See **Becket**)

Cornish chough

Cornucopia The horn of plenty is always so termed.

Coronel (See **Cronal**)

Coronets There are two types of coronet, crest coronets and coronets of rank. Crest coronets, such as the ducal coronet and coronet composed of fleurs-de-lis, sometimes called an 'ancient coronet', are ornamental circlets used by some families in addition to, or more usually, in lieu of a wreath. Recently there was a vogue for crest coronets consisting of a circlet set about with a variety of charges, such as roses, garbs, leaves, etc. So frequently were these used that today the kings of arms will seldom grant them. Coronets of rank are worn by various members of the royal family and by peers of the realm at coronations. They are depicted above their arms in an achievement of arms. These coronets are of silver gilt, are chased as jewelled (except for the coronet of a baron which has a plain circlet) and some have pearls, which are shown as silver balls. They may be shown either with or without the velvet cap, turned up with ermine and having a gold tassel on the top. If the cap is omitted care should be taken not to show the ermine band beneath the rim of the coronet. The coronet of the heir-apparent to the Crown consists of four crosses formy and four fleurs-de-lis set alternately about a rim studded with jewels with a single arch adorned with pearls and supporting in the centre an orb. The form of this coronet was ordained by King Charles II, as was that of the younger brothers and sisters of the sovereign. Their coronet is like that of the heir-apparent but without the arch. Children of the heir-apparent substitute two strawberry leaves for two of the crosses formy. Other grandchildren or children of younger brothers of the sovereign have a coronet composed of four crosses formy and four strawberry leaves. Children of daughters of the sovereign have a coronet composed of four fleurs-de-lis and four strawberry leaves. Duke's coronets have eight strawberry leaves on the rim, marquesses' have four interspersed with four pearls slightly raised. Earls have eight strawberry leaves alternating with eight pearls raised on high points. Viscounts have sixteen small pearls set about the rim and barons six larger pearls.

Ducal or crest coronet

Ancient coronet

Baron's coronet

Viscount's coronet

Earl's coronet

Marquess's coronet

Duke's coronet

Cost A diminutive of the bend, normally found in pairs and called 'cottises'.

Cotises (also **Cottises, Costs, Cottizes** or **Cottices**) Narrow bendlets placed on either side of a bend, which is then said to be cottised. Although the cost or cotise was originally a diminutive of the bend, other ordinaries such as the fess and pale can be cotised. If two cotises are shown on either side of the ordinary the term 'double cotised' is used. 'Treble cotised' is also possible, but only just.

Fess cottised

Couchant Describes a beast when lying down with head up.

Crest of a
lion couchant

Couché (also **Couched**) Describes a shield when shown aslant in an achievement of arms. It is purely an artistic conceit to depict arms in this way. It was often employed in the fifteenth century and has enjoyed a measure of popularity this century.

Counter A prefix meaning opposite or reverse. 'Counter-rampant' means rampant to the sinister; 'counter-embattled' – embattled on both sides; two animals counter-passant are passant in opposite directions.

Counterchanged (also **Interchanged** and **Counter-coloured**) A popular device by which a shield is divided by a partition line, the colours or metals on one side of it being reversed on the other side.

Per pale argent
and sable on a
fess between
three roundels
three lozenges
counterchanged

Counter-potent (See **Potent**)
Counter-quarterly (See **Quarterings**)
Counter-vair (See **Vair**)
Countess The title of the wife of an earl or that of a woman who holds an earldom in her own right.

Couped Cut off cleanly. Ordinaries are said to be 'couped' when they are cut off before reaching the edge of the shield.

A fess couped
between three
lions' heads
couped

Couple-close A diminutive of the chevron borne in pairs. The term is rarely used; if a chevron has a diminutive on either side of it, it is usually termed 'cotised'.

Courant (also **Current**) Running at full speed. A horse courant is usually shown with fore-legs stretched in front and hind-legs together in the rear – anatomically impossible but heraldically acceptable.

Courtesy titles Styles accorded to children of peers by the courtesy of the Crown. Sons of dukes and marquesses use the style 'lord', their daughters, and those of an earl, 'lady' before their Christian names. The sons of earls and sons and daughters of viscounts and barons are styled 'honourable'. The eldest son of a duke, marquess or earl takes his father's second title by courtesy, but is not a peer and so does not use a peer's armorial insignia.

Coward (also **Cowed**) A beast with its tail between its hind-legs.

Crampet (also **Chape** and **Boteroll**) The metal tip on the end of a scabbard.

Crampon (also **Cramp**) A piece of metal used by builders to strengthen a building. The straight variety with a pointed hook at the end rather than the usual 'S' type are invariably depicted.

Two crampons
in saltire

Crane   (See **Heron**)
Crenellated   (also **Crenellé**) (See **Embattled**)
Crescent A half-moon with the horns pointing upwards. If the horns point to the dexter it is an 'increscent', if to the sinister, a 'decrescent', and if to the base it is 'a crescent reversed'. It is the mark of a second son.

A decrescent,
an increscent
and a crescent

Crest An hereditary device, modelled onto the top of the helm and part of an achievement of arms. (See Introduction, page 11).
Crest coronet   (See **Coronets**)
Crested   (See **Partition, Lines of** and **Comb**)
Cri de guerre A war cry. Many Scottish families have a *cri de guerre* which is placed in a scroll above the crest. A number of mottoes originated as war cries.
Crined A term used to refer to the hair of man or beast. If, say, an unicorn has a red beard, mane, and tufts

it is simpler to blazon it 'crined gules' than 'bearded maned and tufted gules'.

Cronal (also **Spear cronal** and **Coronel**) The deeply scalloped head of a tournament spear resembling a crown.

Cronal

Crosier (also **Crozier**) The pastoral staff of a bishop or abbot. In continental heraldry the crosier, when used as abbatial insignia, usually has a sudarium or veil attached beneath the crook.

Crosier

Cross An ordinary consisting of a broad cross throughout. A field divided 'per cross' is termed 'quarterly'. Some authors state that there are over three hundred varieties of cross. Here some of the better known types of cross are illustrated.

Crosslet (See **Cross**)

Cross-wise In the form of a cross. The term 'in cross' is more usual.

Cross avellane

Cross parted
and fretty

Cross
quarter pierced

Cross bourdonny

Cross voided

Cross bottony
or trefly

Cross calvary

Cross clechy

Cross crosslet

Cross crosslet
fitched

Cross fleuretty

Cross pointed

Cross formy
or paty

Cross fourché

Cross gammadion,
fylfoot
or swastika

Maltese cross

Cross moline

Passion, Long or
Latin cross

Cross patonce

Patriarchal
cross

Cross pommel

Cross potent

Cross recercely

Cross tau or St
Anthony's cross

Crown The conventional representation of the Royal Crown (sometimes also called the Imperial Crown) is a stylized version of St Edward's Crown. It is composed of a gold circlet on which are four crosses formy, one and two halves being visible, and four fleurs-de-lis, two being shown. The circlet is garnished with pearls and five large jewels; in the centre is a sapphire, flanked by two emeralds, with two rubies at the outer edges. From the crosses rise two gold arches. On the outer two nine, and on the centre arch five pearls are shown. The arches support a mound or orb, often shown as being green, on which is a gold cross formy ornamented with pearls. The actual delineation of the crown varies with the whim of the sovereign but the basic form of the present Royal Crown has been much the same since the end of the seventeenth century.

Various forms of coronet are known as crowns rather than coronets and are used as charges, adornments or in place of the wreath beneath the crest. These crowns are best described by the illustrations.

Royal crown   Ancient crown   Astral crown

Celestial crown   Eastern crown   King of arms's crown

Naval crown   Palisado crown   Crown vallary

Two types of Mural crown

Crowned When this expression is used a ducal coronet is implied unless some other form of crown or coronet is mentioned.

Crusily (also **Crusilly, Crusilé, Crucily** and **Crusuly**) Semy of cross crosslets; 'crusily fitchy' is semy of cross crosslets fitched.

Cubit arm An arm couped below the elbow. (See **Arm**)

Cuffed Applied to the cuff when of a different tincture from the sleeve.

Cuise (See **Quise, à la**)

Cuppa I only know of one example of this variety of potent (q.v.), namely in the arms granted to John White in 1750, which are illustrated. It is what in German heraldry is called succinctly – *verschobenes gegensturzkruckenfeh.*

Fess Cuppa

Current (See **Courant**)

Cushion (also **Oreiller** and **Pillow**) These are usually square with tassels at each corner. Lozenge-shaped cushions are also found but if they are of any other shape then they should be so blazoned. The cushion is not easily distinguished from the wool pack (q.v.), which is depicted as a crude cushion.

Cypher A monogram. The cyphers of members of the royal family are widely used and are normally recorded at the College of Arms.

Dagger   This is drawn very like a sword and is often indistinguishable from it. Ideally the blade of the dagger should be drawn short and sharply pointed.

Damasked   (See **Diapered**)

Dance   A term used to describe a fess dancetty. It was often found in early blazon and has been used in the blazon of some recent grants of arms.

Dance

Dancetty   (also **Dancetté** and **Dancy**) A line of partition similar to indented but showing only a few deep indentations. For example, a chief dancetty usually shows three indentations. A fess dancetty is also called a 'dance'. (See **Partition, Lines of**)

Danish Axe   Similar to the battle axe but with a plain curved haft.

David, Shield of   The two blue interlaced triangles which form the ancient symbol known as the shield, or sometimes star, of David are invariably blazoned as interlaced triangles and are often found in the arms of Jews and Jewish institutions.

Debruised   (also **Surmounted, Suppressed and Oppressed**) A term used to describe a charged field overlaid by an ordinary or subordinary. When one charge is laid over another the term 'surmounted' is often employed. The terms 'suppressed' and 'oppressed' are virtually obsolete.

Dechaussé   (See **Dismembered**)

Decollé*   (also **Decollated**) Decapitated.

Decrescent   A crescent whose horns face the sinister. (See **Crescent**)

Deer When this generic term is used without qualification the stag or red-deer is depicted, but often the actual genus and sex of deer is indicated by the blazon. Those most commonly used are buck, hart, hind, reindeer, roebuck and the actual stag. Certain special terms are applied to beasts of the deer family. The antlers are called 'attires', the horns themselves 'tines'. A running deer is 'in full chase', 'full course' or 'at speed'; when passant 'trippant'; when statant guardant he is 'at gaze'; when lying down, 'lodged'; and when salient, 'springing'.

Defamed* Having no tail.

Degrees (See **Grieces**)

Delf (also **Delve** and **Delph**) A square billet. In heraldic fantasy a delf in the centre of the shield is said to be the abatement for one who revoked a challenge.

Demembered (See **Dismembered**)

Demi A prefix applied to any charge which has been bisected and of which only one half (usually the upper, front or dexter portion) is shown.

Demi vol (See **Vol**)

Dented An old term used to describe the teeth of a beast when of a different tincture from the body.

Descent, Arms of (See **Arms of descent**)

Devisal of arms Originally a synonym for a grant or gift of arms, this expression has recently been given a special meaning. It refers to arms designed by the kings of arms for American corporations who petition them for such a devisal. It is not, of course, a grant of arms, as the kings of arms have no authority to grant arms to American corporations; it is simply a formal designing of arms, permitted by the Earl Marshal and agreed to by the governor of the state in which the devisee is situate.

Dexter The right-hand side of the shield from the point of view of the bearer, but the left as observed from the front. Unless otherwise mentioned all charges, whether in arms or crest, which are capable of facing a given direction, face the dexter. The dexter is the more important side of the shield, taking precedence over the sinister. (See **Points of the shield**)

Diamond   Used for sable when blazoning by jewels. (See **Jewels**)

Diapered (also **Damasked**) Patterned. A way of relieving plain surfaces by covering them with designs or patterns, usually in darker and lighter shades of the same tincture. Whilst diapering is a matter of artistic licence, the artist should be careful not to diaper in such a way as to allow confusion with a charged surface.

Difference, Marks of   Small marks added to arms to distinguish the male members of a family one from the other. The eldest son has a label, the second a crescent, the third a mullet, the fourth a martlet, the fifth an annulet, the sixth a fleur-de-lis, the seventh a rose, the eighth a cross moline and the ninth an octofoil. The second son of a second son will have a crescent on a crescent and his third son a mullet on a crescent on a crescent and so forth. The absurdity of such a system is manifest and consequently it is more honoured in the breach than the observance, being invoked only where the use of a mark of difference is really necessary; for example if two brothers were both Knights of the Garter, the younger would need to difference his crest and banner, as there would be no other way of telling whose was whose. In Scotland marks of difference are obligatory and are bestowed by Lyon King of Arms when arms are matriculated. Members of the royal family are granted marks of difference, now always shown on labels of three or five points, by the sovereign. These are not hereditary. (See **Cadency**)

Dimidiation   An old method of impalement whereby the two coats to be joined were bisected, the dexter half of one being joined to the sinister half of the other. The inevitable mutilation of both coats and the fanciful charges which it sometimes produced made the life of this form of impalement a short but merry one.

Diminutive Narrow version of an ordinary, seldom borne singly and seldom charged. These terms were not used in early blazon: a shield charged with three chevrons was so blazoned; they were not termed chevronels. The bar and the baton are the only two diminutives which have a decent antiquity. It is a hopeful sign that these niceties of blazon (like lioncels for little lions) are now seldom used by the kings of arms.

Disarmed A creature without its offensive weapons, such as claws, beak, teeth, horns etc., is said to be disarmed.

Dismembered (also **Dechaussé** or **Demembered**) A creature whose limbs are severed but are still depiced, the field just appearing between the body and severed limbs. 'Couped at the joints' is another and more usual way of blazoning such an unfortunate beast.

Display arms (See **Bear arms**)

Displayed Used of a bird whose wings are outspread, the tips pointing upwards. Some centuries ago, and again today, the term is used indifferently whether the tips of the wings point up or down; but there was a time when, if the points were downwards, the expression 'displayed wings inverted' was used. In very early blazon the eagle, as it was invariably shown displayed, was simply blazoned an 'eagle'.

Distilling Shedding drops; thus a severed head distils drops of blood and a woman's breast distils drops of milk.

Distinction, Marks of Just as marks of cadency are referred to as 'marks of difference', so marks of bastardy or marks added to show absence of blood relationship (as in adoption or in arms granted by virtue of a Royal Licence) are usually called 'marks of distinction'.

Distinguished Service Cross A decoration instituted in 1901 (formerly called the Conspicuous Service Cross) to reward services before the enemy. It is awarded only to officers of certain rank in the Royal Navy and Royal

Marines. A representation of it may be suspended beneath the shield.

Distinguished Flying Cross   A decoration instituted in 1918. It is awarded to officers and warrant officers in the Royal Air Force for exceptional valour, courage and devotion to duty when flying in active operations against the enemy. The Air Force Cross, which was instituted at the same time, is awarded for similar services, but not in active operations. Representations of these crosses may be suspended beneath the shield.

Distinguished Service Order   Instituted in 1886, this order has only one class. It is awarded to serving officers in the armed forces and merchant navy for distinguished service in combat. Companions may display it beneath their shield of arms.

Divorce   For the arms of a divorced woman, see **Women's arms**.

Dolphin   The heraldic dolphin is always shown embowed, has a pronounced beak and fins and usually shows a tongue. If its position is not blazoned, 'naiant' is understood, but dolphins are also found 'haurient' and 'urinant'.

Crest of a
dolphin

Domestic prelate to the Pope   A domestic prelate may ensign his arms with a violet ecclesiastical hat having six tassels pendent on either side.

Dominion, Arms of   (See **Arms of dominion**)

Dormant   Sleeping; applied to creatures who are couchant but with head down and eyes closed.

Double arched (also **Double enarched**) (See **Arched**)

Double-headed With two heads. When applied to the eagle, as it generally is, the term implies that one head looks to the dexter and the other to the sinister.

Double-quaterfoil (See **Octofoil**)

Double-queued Having two tails. Care should be taken to show two tails emerging from the base of the spine so as to avoid confusion with the queue fourchée. (See **Queue** and **Queue fourchée**)

Double-tressure Two tressures drawn very close together When a double-tressure is flory counter-flory, as in the Royal Arms of Scotland, the fleurs-de-lis interspersing the two tressures are not shown in the space between the two.

Arms of
Scotland, with
double tressure
flory counter-flory

Doubled In describing a mantling this term means 'lined with'. A mantling gules and argent would be blazoned, 'mantled gules doubled argent'. The terms 'turned' and 'lined' are also found, but are not used today.

Dovetailed (See **Partition, Lines of**)

Dragon Originally indistinguishable from the wyvern, the dragon has for long been shown as a wyvern with four legs. Today the tongue and tail are usually shown barbed but this has not always been so. Essentially it is a scaly monster with bat-like wings and an eagle's claws. In recent years Chinese dragons have appeared but they are always so blazoned.

Dragon passant
on a mount. A
royal badge
for Wales

Ducal coronet When this term is used, a coronet composed of four (three visible) strawberry leaves on a rim chased as jewelled is always intended. It is sometimes just called a 'crest coronet' (a description currently in vogue), as this is its principal use. When any creature is said to be 'crowned' or 'gorged with a coronet' the ducal coronet is understood. The inclusion of such a coronet in a crest or shield of arms is no indication of rank or even of illustrious ancestry, however much some of those who bear this charge would have us believe otherwise. (See **Coronet**)

Duchess The title of the wife of a duke or that of a woman who holds a dukedom in her own right.

Duke The first and highest rank in the peerage. The title was not used in England until 1337, when Edward the Black Prince was created Duke of Cornwall. (See **Peers** and **Coronet**)

Dunghill cock The common farmyard cock. (See **Cock**)

Eagle   The eagle is usually drawn in a stylized manner, especially when shown 'displayed', its usual position. However, the eagle is also found 'rising' (particularly in crests), 'close', 'volant', 'trussing' or 'preying upon' another creature and 'stooping'. When an eagle's wings are displayed and the tips point downwards they are sometimes, but not invariably, blazoned 'inverted'.

Eagle displayed

Eagle displayed,
wings inverted

Eaglet   When more than one eagle was charged on a shield the small eagles were sometimes termed 'eaglets', but this pointless diminutive is not now used.

Eale   (See **Yale**)

Earl   The third rank in the peerage. The title was used by the Norman kings but is of Saxon origin. (See **Peer** and **Coronet**)

Earl Marshal   The great Officer of State who is responsible for state ceremonies. He is also the hereditary judge in the Court of Chivalry and has jurisdiction over the officers of arms and matters of heraldry, honour and precedence. The title, which was originally simply 'Marshal' but is now 'Earl Marshal and Hereditary Marshal of England', is vested in the Duke of Norfolk as male heir of John Howard, the first Duke.

Eastern crown   A crown of eight high points (five of which are seen). (See **Crown**)

Eau   (See **Goutty**)

Ecclesiastical hat   A domed or sometimes boater-like hat with a wide brim from which depends on either side a varying number of tassels on cords. This hat ensigns the arms of Roman Catholic prelates and clergy, and the colour of the hat and the number of tassels denote the rank of the bearer. The official use of these hats in English heraldry was detailed in 1967 in an Earl Marshal's Warrant. (See: **Archbishop, Abbot** (also for Abbot Nullius Dioceseos), **Bishop, Canon, Cardinal, Domestic prelate, Priest, Privy Chamberlain** (also for Privy Chaplain), **Protonotary Apostolic** (also for Vicar Apostolic and Prefect Apostolic) and **Religious Superior**).

Ecclesiastical
hat

Egrentyne   A monster which appears to occur only once in heraldry, namely as a supporter to the arms of Lord Fastolfe. It has a dragon-like head, a long body, cloven hooves on its fore-legs and webbed back feet and a long hairy tail. It is demonstrably masculine.

Elevated   This refers to wings when the points are upwards. The term is now seldom used.

Eightfoil   (See **Octofoil**)

Embattled   (also **Imbattled, Battled, Crenellated** and **Crenelle**) (See **Partition, Lines of** and **Bretessed**)

Emblazon   To paint in correct colours; not to be confused with 'to blazon' which is to describe.

Embowed   Bent; most often used of fish and human arms which are flexed at the elbow. (See **Arm**). A chevron embowed is one which has concave limbs.

Embrued   (also **Imbrued**) Spattered or dripping with blood. Often used of blood-stained weapons.

Emerald   Used for vert when blazoning by jewels. (See **Jewels**)

Enaluron   A term occasionally used when blazoning a

bordure charged with birds.

Enarched (See **Arched**)

Encircled (also **Voluted** and **Involved**) Used of serpents when coiled so as to form a circle. 'Encircled by' has its usual meaning. (See **Enfile**)

Encoutrant (See **Respectant**)

Endorsed (See **Addorsed**)

Enfield A monster of doubtful origin and antiquity which occurs in several coats. It has the head, hindquarters and tail of a fox, the body of a dog and eagle's claws.

Enfield passant

Enfile To surround or encircle. The three feathers in the badge of the heir-apparent to the Crown are 'enfiled by' a coronet.

Enflamed (also **Inflamed**, **Flamant** and **Fired**) Applied to anything which is flaming.

England When the expression 'of England' is used in a blazon it means 'of the royal arms of England' (i.e. gules, three lions passant guardant in pale or). A 'bordure of England' is a red bordure charged with an indefinite number of gold lions passant guardant. A 'lion of England' is one of the royal lions.

Englishman's head (See **Head**)

Engrailed (See **Partition, Lines of**)

Enhanced (also **Hausé** or **Haussé**) Applied to an ordinary (most frequently the bend) when raised above its normal position.

Three bendlets
enhanced

Ensign   A type of flag. The term is now applied to the White Ensign (a naval flag); the Red Ensign (a flag which can be worn by British-owned craft); the Blue Ensign (a government flag); the Royal Air Force Ensign (an RAF flag); and the Civil Ensign (similar to the Red Ensign but used in connection with aeroplanes). It is always pronounced 'ens'n'.

Ensigned   A charge which has a crown, coronet or similar decoration placed above it is said to be 'ensigned' by whatever is over it.

Entire   (See **Throughout**)

Entoured   Placed around: usually this particular term refers to a shield which is encircled by a decorative wreath. (See **Encircled**)

Entayre*   A term used when blazoning a bordure charged with inanimate objects.

Enty*   Parted per chevron.

Enurny*   A term used when blazoning a bordure charged with lions.

Environed   Encircled by. (See **Encircled**)

Episcopal staff (also **Archiepiscopal cross**)   A staff ensigned by a cross. It is used as insignia by Roman Catholic bishops as an alternative to the crozier. As a charge it occurs in the arms of the see of Canterbury and elsewhere but in this context is usually termed an 'archiepiscopal cross'.

Episcopal staff

Equipped Fully armed; a term occasionally used as a synonym for 'armed cap-à-pie' for a man or 'caparisoned' for a horse.

Eradicated Torn out by the roots; generally used of trees where the roots are shown in detail.

Erased Torn off roughly so as to leave a jagged edge. This term is usually applied to parts of living creatures rudely severed from their bodies. If a charge is blazoned as being erased of a different tincture from the charge itself then it is shown as in the illustration.

Crest of a
lion's head
erased

Erased of a
different
tincture

Erect A term applied to a charge shown upright when it would not normally be so depicted.

Ermine One of the two principal furs used in heraldry. It consists of black ermine tails (drawn in a variety of stylized forms) on a white field. Purists argue, and with some justification, that the field must indeed be white and not silver, which in any case is seldom used, as it represents fur and not metal. An ermine spot can be borne as a charge.

Four types of
ermine spot

Ermines A fur which is the reverse of ermine, consisting of white tails on black.

Erminites* A fur which is the same as ermine except that there are two red hairs in the tail of each ermine spot.

Erminois A fur consisting of black ermine spots on a gold field.

Escallop The scallop shell. That shown in heraldry is normally the back of the convex left shell with the point in chief and the 'ears' showing. The scallop was not only the symbol of St James of Compostella but was favoured by pilgrims as an invaluable general service utensil. It was carried by a cord which passed through two holes in the 'beak' of the shell, which holes are sometimes found in heraldic representations. It is a very popular misconception that the incidence of a scallop shell in a coat of arms argues an ancestor who went on a crusade. In very ancient coats it could mean this but usually there is no connection.

Escallop

Escarbuncle (also **Carbuncle** and **Escarboucle**) Ornamental spokes normally eight and usually terminating in fleurs-de-lis) radiating from a centre boss. Originally this was probably a shield boss, rather than either a buckle or a stylized representation of the precious stone, as some writers suggest. The number of rays, especially if other than eight, is sometimes mentioned in the blazon.

Escarbuncle

Escartellé (See **Partition, Lines of**)

Escroll (also **Scroll**) A ribbon or scroll usually bearing a motto.

Escutcheon (also **Scutcheon** and **Scotcheon**) A shield. When a shield is borne as a charge it is normally termed an 'escutcheon', or 'inescutcheon'. An Escutcheon of Pretence is a small shield containing the arms of an heraldic heiress, which is placed in the centre of her husband's arms in their marital achievement.

Espallade crown* Palisado crown. (See **Crown**)

Esquire Originally a knight's attendant and shield-bearer. Today, as nobody knows who is and who is not an esquire, it is used everywhere to avoid giving offence. In fact relatively few people are entitled to the designation. Those who are fall into three main classes: 1 esquires by inheritance (e.g. the eldest sons of knights); 2 esquires by patent (e.g. heralds, who are so styled in their Letters Patent of creation); and 3 esquires during tenure of office (e.g. justices of the peace when serving in that office). An esquire's helmet is a steel helmet with closed visor facing dexter. The term 'esquire' is sometimes used to describe a single gyron (q.v.).

Estate, Cap of (See **Chapeau**)

Estoil A star of six points drawn with wavy lines like a starfish. If other than six points are shown the number should be blazoned. In Tudor times estoils were sometimes called 'stars' and often irradiated but today an irradiated estoil would have to be blazoned accordingly.

Estoil

Extraordinary Officer of Arms (See **Officer of Arms**)

Falchion   A broad-bladed sword, the front edge being curved, the back straight. (See **Scimitar** and **Seax**)

Falchion

Falcon   In falconry this term is used to refer to the long-winged birds, such as gyrfalcons, peregrines, merlins, etc., whilst the term 'hawk' is reserved for goshawks, sparrowhawks and short-winged birds. In heraldry, although both terms are found in blazon, the artistic representation is usually identical. Falcons and hawks are generally belled and also often jessed, that is with short leather straps attached to the legs.

False   A rare term meaning voided. An orle is sometimes called a 'false escutcheon'.

Fan   (also **Vane**) Originally the only fan known to armory was the winnowing fan borne by the Septvans family as a canting charge. However, since the Fanmakers' Company of London now uses a ladies' fan, albeit without authority, a distinction should perhaps be made in the blazon. Some early helmets were crested by a fan. In a few instances these were later used as the definitive armorial crest. The crest of the City of London is a dragon's wing, which almost certainly evolved from a non-armorial, decorative fan crest.

Fasces   An axe within a bundle of rods. It was the symbol of magisterial authority in the Roman Empire and is often found in the arms of those having judicial authority today.

Fasces

Feathers Various types of feather are used, the most common being those of the ostrich and peacock. If the quill of a feather is of a different tincture from the feather itself, it should be blazoned 'quilled' or 'penned' of the appropriate colour.

Feathered (See **Flighted**)

Fer-de-moline (also **Fer-de-mouline**) (See **Millrind**)

Ferrated* Semy of horseshoes.

Fess (also **Fesse**) An ordinary consisting of a broad horizontal band drawn across the centre of the shield.

Fess

Fess point The centre of the shield. (See **Points of the Shield**)

Fesswise Lying in the direction of the fess.

Fetterlock (also **Fetlock**) A type of lock used to hobble horses. It is normally shown closed, but when, as in the falcon and fetterlock badge of Edward IV, it is open it should be so blazoned.

Falcon and
fetterlock,
badge of
Edward IV

Field The surface of the shield on which the charges are placed. It may be plain, patterned or divided.

Figured Decorated with a human face. The term is seldom used.

File (See **Label**)

Fillet A diminutive of the chief, drawn as a bar enhanced and rarely, if ever, used.

Fimbriated Edged. The red cross of England in the Union Flag is fimbriated argent so as to avoid placing a red cross on a blue field. There is really little, if any, visual difference between 'a cross gules fimbriated argent' and 'a cross argent thereon another gules'.

Finned Referring to the fins of fishes when of a different tincture from the body.

Fire ball Similar to a grenade but with fire issuing from top, bottom and both sides.

Fire ball

Fired (See **Enflamed**)

Fish Almost every variety of common fish is to be found in heraldry, often to effect a pun on the name of the bearer of the arms. If a fish is swimming horizontally it is termed 'naiant', if erect with head in chief, 'haurient', and if diving downwards, 'urinant' or 'uriant'.

Fitched (also **Fitchy** and **Fitché**) Pointed at the foot. Usually applied to crosses where the lower limb is replaced by a point. If a point is added to the lower limb, it is termed 'fitched at the foot'. (See **Cross**)

Flag A generic term used only when no particular variety of flag is intended. (See **Banner, Ensign, Gonfannon, Guidon, Pennon, Pennoncelle** and **Standard**.)

Flamant (See **Enflamed**)

Flames of fire   Usually depicted as a ball of flame having six tongues.

Flasque*   Said by Gerard Leigh (1591) to be a diminutive of a flaunch but this would seem to be an impossible pedantry.

Flaunches   (also **Flanches, Flasques** and **Flanques**) Two arcs of circles on either side of the shield. They are always borne in pairs. Some writers hold that flasques are narrow flaunches and that voiders are even narrower but these distinctions do not seem to have got further than the textbooks.

Flaunches

Fleam   (also **Fleme** and **Flegme**) An ancient form of lancet. It makes an attractive charge and is often used in the arms of surgeons and generally in medical heraldry.

Fleam

Flected   (See **Flexed**)

Fleece   The fleece of a horned ram is always depicted as if suspended from a hook, being encircled by a band to which is attached a ring. A fleece is often 'banded' and 'ringed' of different tinctures from the fleece itself.

Fleece

Flesh pot Usually depicted as a round cauldron with three legs.

Fleur-de-lis (also **Fleur-de-lys**) A stylized form of lily, although some writers ascribe other origins to this popular and ancient charge. The plural is 'fleurs-de-lis' and it can be drawn in a variety of ways. It is the mark of a sixth son.

Three types of
fleur-de-lis

Fleury (See **Flory**)

Fleuretty (also **Floretty**) Sometimes a plain cross with fleurs-de-lis issuant from the ends of the traverses is so described, but such a cross is also sometimes blazoned 'flory' or 'fleury'. Frequently no distinction is made between the cross flory and cross patonce, although some draw a distinction between the ways in which the traverse of the two crosses are drawn (see **Cross**). This term is also applied to a field or charge which is semy-de-lis, but then the fleurs-de-lis are small and very close together.

Flexed (also **Flected**) Bent, used principally of the limbs of the body.

Flighted (also **Feathered**) Referring to the feathers of an arrow.

Floretty (See **Fleuretty**)

Flory (also **Fleury**) Used of charges terminating in or ornamented with fleurs-de-lis. (See **Cross**)

Flory counter-flory (also **Fleury counter-fleury**) Used of charges decorated with fleurs-de-lis alternately on either side. The double tressure in the arms of Scotland is 'flory counter-flory'. (See **Double-tressure**)

Flotant Floating, with reference to either flags or

ships.

Fluke   The barbed or pointed part of an anchor.

Fluted   Used of a pillar when shown fluted.

Fly   That part of a flag furthest from the mast or hoist.

Foliated   With leaves.

Forcene   (also **Forcené**) Properly used to describe a horse rearing up or salient but it has been incorrectly used on many occasions, even in official blazon, to describe a horse rampant.

Forest bill   (See **Bill**)

Formy   (See **Cross**)

Fountain   A roundel barry wavy (usually of six pieces) argent and azure. It is also called a syke, but the only known instance is in the arms of the family of Sykes, thus making the pun patently obvious. If a natural fountain is intended it must be made clear in the blazon. The arms of Brunner, baronets, contain one such fountain and it is blazoned: 'a fountain playing proper'.

Fountain

Fourché   Forked; this term is frequently used to describe a tail which divides into two. (See **Cross**)

Fox's mask   A fox's face caboshed is so termed.

Fracted   Broken.

France   A bordure of France is a blue bordure charged with gold fleurs-de-lis (from the old arms of France). A label of France is a blue label, each point charged with three fleurs-de-lis or else the whole label is semy-de-lis. In the same way a canton of France would be a canton of the arms of France. The blazon should specify whether it is

France ancient (semy-de-lis) or France modern (charged with three fleurs-de-lis).

Fraise (also **Frase, Fraze, Frasier**) A synonym for the cinquefoil, meaning the flower of the strawberry plant. It is used to make a pun in the blazon of the arms of various families of Fraser, which contain three cinquefoils.

Fret A mascle interlaced by a bendlet and a bendlet sinister. It is normally shown throughout except when more than one is borne. As the family of Harington bears sable, a fret argent, it is sometimes called a Harington knot. (See **Knot**)

A fret with a
chief fretty

Fretty Bendlets and bendlets sinister interlaced to form a lozengy pattern like a loose net or trellis. If this net is formed by palets and bars, it is termed 'square fretty'.

Fructed Bearing fruit. An oak tree with acorns would be described as 'fructed'.

Fumant Emitting smoke.

Furnished A horse fully caparisoned (q.v.) is said to be furnished or completely furnished.

Furs The two principal furs used in heraldry are ermine and vair. The former has variants: ermines, erminites, erminois and pean. The latter also has variants: vairé, vair counter, potent and counter-potent. For details see under the various headings. In theory a fur may lie on either a colour of a metal, which likewise may be placed on a fur. In practice a king of arms would be unlikely to grant, for example, a silver charge on an ermine field.

Fusil This is really a distaff but is shown as a long

narrow lozenge. Actual fusils are occasionally found.

Fusilly Similar to lozengy (q.v.) but the lines bendy and bendy sinister which form the pattern are nearer the horizontal, thus forming narrower, more fusil-like compartments.

Fylfot Another name for the Cross Gammadion or Swastika. (See **Cross**)

Gad   (also **Steel-gad,** or **Gad of steel**) A plate of steel often drawn like a billet.

Galley   (See **Lymphad**)

Galtrap   (See **Caltrap**)

Gamb   (See **Jamb**)

Game Lion   As granted to Thomas Gardiner in 1557 this monster would seem to consist of a griffin's body with a dragon's wings and tail.

Gammadion   (See **Cross**)

Garb   A sheaf of wheat, unless the blazon specifies some other type of grain. It is always banded, but the band is not blazoned unless of a different tincture from the garb.

Garb

Gardant   (See **Guardant**)

Garland   (See **Chaplet**)

Garnished   Used to describe the decoration on charges such as pieces of armour, bugle, horns etc., when of a different tincture from the charge itself. It is sometimes used in connection with vesture but in this context 'purfled' is the more usual term. (See **Purfled**)

Garter   A circular riband with buckle and strap pendent. 'Garter' or 'gartier' is also given in textbooks as a diminutive of the bend but it has seldom, if ever, been officially used.

Garter

Garter King of Arms   The principal English king of arms. The office was instituted by King Henry V in 1415, William Bruges being the first to hold it. Garter (as he is generally known) has no province but is chairman of the Chapter of the English officers of arms. He grants supporters, arms to peers, signs all grants of arms together with the appropriate provincial kings and has special duties in connection with the Order of the Garter. (See Introduction, page 8)

Garter, Order of the   The Most Noble Order of the Garter was instituted by King Edward III circa 1348. It now consists of the sovereign, the Prince of Wales, twenty-four knights companions and such lineal descendants of King George I as may be elected and such extra knights as may be admitted by special statutes. St George is the patron saint of the order. Knights are entitled to a grant of supporters, to encircle their arms with the collar with badge pendent and with the garter on which the motto of the order, *'Honi Soit Qui Mal y Pense'*, is inscribed. The badge shows St George killing the dragon. That attached to the collar is known as 'the George'; the 'Lesser George' is similar but is pendent from a blue ribbon worn over the left shoulder. The chapel of the order is St George's Chapel, Windsor, where the knights' banners and crests can be seen above their stalls and where there is a magnificent collection of stall plates.

Gate   A gate is usually represented in the manner illustrated. The number of bars is usually not less than three nor more than five.

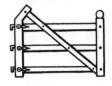

Gate

Gauntlet Gauntlets of various periods and styles are found but the blazon rarely specifies which particular type of gauntlet should be shown. It should be stated whether a gauntlet is dexter or sinister. If the palm is shown it is best to blazon it 'apaumé', though some hold that this is how it should normally appear.

Dexter   Sinister
gauntlet apaumé   gauntlet apaumé

Ged A term sometimes used in place of 'pike' or 'lucy'; usually, as in the arms of Ged of that Ilk, when a pun is intended.

Gem ring A ring set with one stone.

Gemel (See **Bar gemel** and **Collar gemel**)

Genet A mammal belonging to the civet family. The word is also sometimes used of the broom plant or *planta genista.*

Gentleman This term is applied to one who bears arms by inheritance or grant (a gentleman of coat-armour) or one who, to put it in a nutshell, is eligible for a grant of arms. A gentleman bears arms in the same way as an esquire, using a steel helm with closed visor facing the dexter.

George Cross A decoration instituted in 1940 to reward acts of the greatest heroism or most conspicuous courage in circumstances of extreme danger. It is awarded to civilians as well as members of the armed forces. A representation of it may be suspended beneath the shield.

George, The For this and the Lesser George, see **Garter, Order of the**.

Geratting* Semy but with the charges strewn over the shield in such a way that none is cut off by the outline of the shield. (See **Sans Nombre**)

Gilly flower (also **Gillie flower**) Many varieties of flower are so called but in heraldry the common pink is usually intended. Outside heraldry it is usually applied to the carnation or cultivated clove and in England is often used of stocks.

Gimmel ring (also **Gimbal ring** and **Gemel ring**) A ring consisting of two or more rings interlaced. (See **Annulet**)

Giraffe (See **Camelopard**)

Glissant Gliding; a term sometimes applied to reptiles.

Globe (also **Sphere**) This term implies the terrestrial globe or sphere, with the outlines of the land masses and the lines of longitude and latitude rather casually indicated. It is usually termed a 'terrestrial globe' rather than simply a 'globe' so as to distinguish it from the celestial sphere, and is often blazoned 'proper', although this is interpreted in a variety of ways. To avoid equivocation it is best never to use the terms 'globe' or 'sphere' unless they are qualified.

Glory (also **Circle of glory, Halo** and **Nimbus**) A synonym for halo which is variously depicted as a roundle, annulet or irradiated cloud. When the glory is behind the head of Christ or type of Christ it is usually embellished with a cross.

Glove The glove is treated in the same way as the gauntlet (q.v.).

Goat The common male goat with horns and beard is always depicted unless the blazon specifies otherwise. For example Assyrian, Indian and Angorra goats are also to be found.

Gobony (also **Gobone** and **Gobonated**) (See **Compony**)

Gold In medieval blazon the term 'gold' was used more frequently than 'or' and in recent years it has often been employed in blazon to avoid repetition.

Golpe A purple roundel is sometimes so termed.

Gonfannon A long flag, suspended from the top and having several tails or streamers.

Gore* A curious charge best described by the illustration overleaf.

Gore sinister

Gorge (See **Gurges**)

Gorged Collared. If a creature is simply blazoned as being gorged, a plain collar is implied. 'Ducally gorged' means gorged with a ducal or crest coronet.

Goutte A drop.

Goutty (also **Goutté**, **Gutty** and **Gutté**) Strewn with drops. Instead of blazoning a field or charge 'goutty argent', 'goutty gules'. etc., more picturesque descriptions are used: 'goutty d'or' (gold drops); 'goutty d'eau' (silver drops); 'goutty de sang' (red drops); 'goutty des larmes' (blue drops); 'goutty de poix' (black drops); 'goutty d'huile' or, rarely, 'goutty d'olive' (green drops). The current fashion in official armory is to use the spelling 'gutty' but the other spellings are all frequently employed.

Goutty

Grady Ascending like steps. The arms of Eastbourne Training College are divided 'per chevron indented grady'.

Per chevron
indented grady

Gradient* Walking slowly like a tortoise.

Grand Quarter One of the main quarterings in a coat of arms; used in contra-distinction to sub-quarterings, which are quarterings within a quartering.

Grant of Arms A bestowal of arms by a competent authority. In England the kings of arms grant arms by Letters Patent under their hands and seals on receipt of a Warrant from the Earl Marshal. In Scotland Lyon King of Arms grants arms. (See Introduction, page 6)

Grappling iron An instrument used in naval engagements to lock two ships together. It is shaped like an anchor but has four flukes.

Gray* A badger; 'brock' is the more usual term.

Grenade (also **Bomb**) A round ball with flames issuing from the top.

Grenade

Greyhound Although the greyhound is an ancient and popular charge, it is drawn as in nature but assumes the usual heraldic postures.

Grieces (also **Greeces** and **Greces**) Steps. Another term is 'degrees' and sometimes the simple word 'steps' is used. When blazoning the cross calvary the number of grieces on which it stands is specified.

Griffin (also **Gryphon**) A monster which has the hind-parts of a lion and the head, breast, claws and wings of an eagle. It also has ears and often a short beard. When the griffin is shown rampant it is blazoned 'segreant'. The male griffin has no wings but rays or spikes protrude from his body.

Male griffin
segreant

Griffin passant

Guardant (also **Gardant**) With the face looking outwards. When blazoning animals the position of the body
is mentioned first, then the position of the head. The lions
of England are 'passant guardant'.

Lion passant
guardant

Guidon Originally a small tapering flag like a small
standard. It was much in evidence in funeral heraldry in
the sixteenth and seventeenth centuries but is not used
today. The modern guidon is a flag used by cavalry
regiments.

Gules The colour red. It is usually pure vermilion. In
engraving vertical lines are used to indicate gules. It is
abbreviated *g.* or *gu*.

Gunstone (See **Pellet**)

Gurges (also **Gorge**) A whirlpool, depicted as shown
in the illustration.

Gurges

Gusset   A charge similar to the pall. When borne sinister it is an abatement for adultery. It was recently granted, in the form shown in the illustration, as an abatement to a Scottish coat, the bearer of which had been judged the guilty party in a divorce case.

Gusset sinister

Gutty   (also **Gutté**) (See **Goutty**)

Guze*   A sanguine roundel is sometimes so termed.

Gyron (also **Esquire**)   Half of a quarter divided by a diagonal line. To make the blazon clear the position of a single gyron or esquire should be noted.

Base Gyron in chief

Gyronny   Divided into wedge-shaped sections by three or more intersecting lines. Normally, when a field or charge is simply blazoned 'gyronny' eight divisions are intended, the division being per saltire and quarterly. If there are six (the division here is per saltire and per fess), ten, twelve or more divisions the blazon must specify how many, but even if there are the usual eight divisions it is wisest to indicate this in the blazon by saying 'gyronny of eight'.

Gyronny

Habited Clothed. Another word frequently used is 'vested'.

Hafted (also **Helved**). Term used to describe the handle of tools and weapons such as spears, axes, hatchets and the like.

Halo (See **Circle of Glory**)

Hamade (also **Hamaide** and **Humet**) A great deal has been written about this charge. It consists of a bar couped at each end, but was originally always borne in threes. There is a dispute as to whether a hamade is properly three couped bars and therefore cannot be borne singly. The adjective humetty (q.v.) is derived from it.

Hamade or hamades

Hammer Various different sorts of hammer occur in heraldry. Unless a specific type is blazoned it is usual to show an ordinary wooden hammer with metal head and ball.

Hand When the human hand is depicted it is normally a dexter hand, couped at the wrist and apaumé, but the blazon should always describe the hand in detail. The badge of all baronets, other than Scottish, is a sinister hand couped at the wrist and apaumé gules shown either as an escutcheon or a canton argent. It is often termed the 'Hand of Ulster', as the original purpose of creating baronets was to help with the colonization of Ulster. (See **Benediction**)

Harboured* (See **Lodged**)

Harington knot (See **Fret** and **Knot**)

Harp Either the plain Celtic variety or an ornamented type may be shown. Different monarchs have preferred different representations of the harp in the Irish quartering of the royal arms. Currently a plain harp or, stringed (with seven strings) argent is used. When a decorated harp is shown a demi-female figure with wings usually forms two sides of the harp.

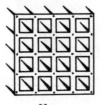

Harpy

Harpy A mythical creature having the body of a vulture but the head and bust of a woman. It is found in the heraldry of Moody of Worcestershire and Wiltshire and derivatively in other families of the same name.

Harrow This agricultural implement is shown as if viewed from above. Both square and triangular harrows are to be found. It is wisest to specify the shape in the blazon.

Harrow

Hart (See **Deer**)

Hat A variety of hats is to be found in heraldry. Whatever the shape they are usually simply blazoned as 'hats' and it is necessary to know the type used by a specific family in order to draw it correctly.

Hatching Properly this means engraving with close parallel lines but loosely it refers to the system of indicating tinctures by hatching and dotting. The illustration shows the method which has been in use in Europe since the late sixteenth century. See also under the various tinctures.

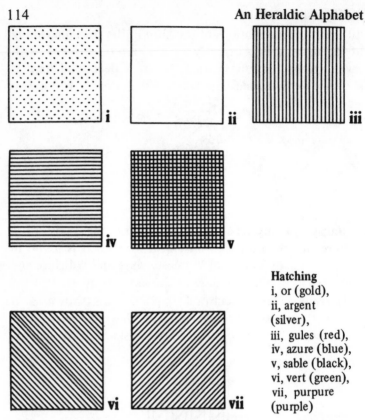

Hatching
i, or (gold),
ii, argent
(silver),
iii, gules (red),
iv, azure (blue),
v, sable (black),
vi, vert (green),
vii, purpure
(purple)

Hatchment The word is a corruption of achievement but has come to be used exclusively for the achievements of deceased persons set forth on large diamond-shaped panels. These were hung outside the house of the defunct during the period of mourning and later were often erected in the parish church. The family motto was often replaced by some apt epithet such as '*Resurgam*' or '*In Caelo Quies*'. If the deceased were a single person, widow or widower the whole of the background of the hatchment was painted black. If the deceased left a widow the sinister half of the background was painted white, if a widower remained then the dexter half was white.

Haurient Applied to a fish when erect with head upwards.

Hausé* (also Haussé) (See Enhanced)

Hawk (See Falcon)

Hawk's bell   A round bell containing a ball.

Hawk's lure   When used as a charge this is generally depicted with the cord embowed as in the illustration.

Hawk's lure

Hayfork (See Shakefork)

Head   Unless the blazon specifies otherwise the head is drawn in profile facing dexter and is couped at the neck. Many varieties of human head are found and as they are frequently simply blazoned 'proper' it is as well to know how they are usually drawn, even though there are no hard and fast rules. A boy's or child's head is that of a young boy with fair hair. An Englishman's head is fair complexioned with fair hair, moustache and usually beard also. A maiden's head is normally shown affronty with long fair hair, and is couped below the bust, but when depicted in this way must be so blazoned. (Sometimes a maiden's hair is blazoned 'dishevelled' as in the grant to William Morgan in 1602.) A blackamoor's head is Negroid with black fuzzy hair. A Saracen's head is swarthy with long, dark hair and beard.A Moor's head, often confused with a blackamoor's head, should really have Arabic features with dark hair and beard. A Saxon's head is usually shown beardless but with fair hair.

Heart   The stylized 'playing-card' type of heart is always used. It is sometimes blazoned a 'human heart' and occasionally a 'body heart'.

Heater shield The heater-shaped shield is that which looks like the base of a flat iron and is probably the most popular vehicle for the emblazonment of arms.

Heaume (See **Helmet**)

Hedgehog (See **Urchin**)

Heir One who has inherited. The term is often used when 'heir-apparent' or 'heir-presumptive' is intended. The heir-apparent is one whose right to succeed is indefeasible by the birth of another. The heir-presumptive is one whose right to succeed will persist only as long as an heir-apparent is not born.

Heiress An heiress or a coheiress in blood is a daughter who has no brothers or whose brothers have died without surviving issue, and whose father is dead. If she marries, her husband bears her paternal arms on an escutcheon of pretence over his own. On her death her arms are transmitted as a quartering to her issue. An heiress in her issue is one who would have been an heiress had she survived the male descendants of her father. For example, if A died leaving three daughters and a son, and that son had a son who had a son who eventually died without issue, the three daughters, although long since dead, would be referred to as coheiresses in their issue because their descendants, on the death of their cousin, would be entitled to quarter the arms of A. Today the term coheiress and heiress are less and less frequently employed, the word heir having become unisexual.

Helmet (also **Helm** and **Heaume**) The helmet is included in an achievement of arms simply because the crest was anciently fixed to the top of it; it is therefore the appropriate vehicle for the display of the crest. In the early seventeenth century rules were devised whereby different types of helm were assigned to different ranks of people. They are as follows: the sovereign and princes of the blood royal have a golden helm, facing outwards and barred. Some books state that there should be six and some ten bars. The fact that in the present approved design of the royal arms the helm has five and in the arms of the Prince of Wales seven bars eloquently illustrates the fact that the Crown can do as it pleases and is not bound by the rulings of either writers or heralds. This helm is also used in the arms of some Commonwealth countries; Malta affords a modern (1964) and Jamaica an ancient (1661) example. Peers have silver helms, facing towards the dexter with gold bars; five are normally shown but there does not appear to be any particular magic in this number. The City of London boasts a peer's helm. Knights and baronets have steel helms shown affronty and with the visor raised. The lining of the helm is usually crimson but this is a rather unimaginative custom and certainly not a rule. Esquires, gentlemen and corporations have steel helms with closed visors facing the dexter. Today considerable latitude is allowed the artist when positioning a helm, so that a knight whose crest faces dexter may have his crest moved a little towards the front and his helm a little towards the dexter, thus making the crest look less ridiculous. The design of the helm is a matter of aesthetics and it is permissible to embellish an esquire's helm with a little gold. Where two helms are shown the dexter helm and crest may be turned round to respect the sinister. Where three helms are depicted the centre one is sometimes shown affronty whilst the other two face inwards, but this is often a bad scheme as it can distort the centre crest. Helmets of various sorts are also used as charges.

Peer's helm   Knight's and baronet's helm   Esquire's and gentleman's helm

Helved   (See **Hafted**)

Hemp-brake   (also **Hemp-bracke** and **Hemp hackle**) An implement used for bruising hemp which occasionally occurs as a charge.

Hemp-brake

Heneage knot   (See **Knot**)

Herald   This term is often used loosely to describe any officer of arms, be he king, herald or pursuivant, but strictly speaking it should refer to the middle rank. (See **Officers of Arms**)

Heraldic antelope   (See Antelope)

Heraldic tyger   (See **Tyger**)

Heraldry   To many this means the study of the art and science of armorial bearings but really it should have wider connotations. (See Introduction, Chapter 1)

Heralds' College   (See **College of Arms**)

Hercules   A wild man or savage, wreathed about the temples and loins and holding a club, is sometimes so described. The dexter supporter of the arms of the Duke of Edinburgh affords an example.

Herisson   (also **Herizon**) A hedgehog. (See **Urchin**)

Hermes, Rod of   (See **Caduceus**)

Heron   (also anciently **Hernshaw** or **Herrynshawe**) Easily confused with the stork and crane. Although ornithologically these three birds belong to different families, artists frequently confuse them and it is often necessary to have special knowledge in order to make a correct blazon. The heron is usually distinguished from the stork by the crest of elongated feathers at the back of the head and the crane is unlike both heron and stork in that it has a longer neck and tail feathers. When shown standing on one leg and grasping a stone in the other claw the crane is said to be 'in its vigilance'.

Heurt (See **Hurt**)

Hilt Strictly speaking the handle of a sword or similar weapon, but in blazon the term usually comprehends both handle and guard. When these are of a different tincture from the sword the term 'hilted' is used. Usually the pommel, the knob on the end of the handle, is of the same tincture as the hilt and the sword is then blazoned as being 'pommelled and hilted' of a given tincture.

Hind A female stag shown without horns. (See **Deer**)

Hippocampus This term is used when blazoning the actual marine sea horse in contra-distinction from the heraldic sea horse. The blazon normally reads 'a sea horse (hippocampus)'. (See **Sea-monsters**)

Hippocampus

Hippogriff* A monster formed by joining the top of a female griffin to the hind-parts of a horse.

Hoist That part of a flag nearest to the mast.

Holy Lamb (See **Paschal Lamb**)

Honorary arms Arms granted by the English kings of arms to people who are not British subjects (but who are descended in the direct, legitimate, male line from a subject of the Crown) are so termed. Should a person entitled by grant or descent to honorary arms become a British subject, his arms would be regarded as equal in every way to those of a natural-born subject of the Crown.

Before a grant of honorary arms is made the prospective grantee must record his English descent in the official records of the College of Arms.

Honourable augmentations (See **Augmentations**)

Honourable ordinaries (See **Ordinaries**)

Honour point A point of the shield which is sited between the fess point and the top of the shield. (See **Points of the shield**)

Hooded Used of a falcon or other hunting bird when the head is masked with a hood. A religious in his habit with his cowl on his head is also so termed.

Hoofed (See **Unguled**)

Horn (See **Bugle horn**)

Horn of plenty (See **Cornucopia**)

Horned Sometimes used when describing the horns of animals other than stags but the term 'armed' is more frequently employed.

Horse The positions adopted by a horse are described in the same way as those of other animals except when it is shown rearing; it is then described as 'forcene'. A horse's head is usually termed a 'nag's head'.

Horseshoe Unless otherwise blazoned the horseshoe is represented as an ordinary shoe (not a racing plate) with the extremities pointing downward, in careless defiance of the not-so-old superstition.

Horseshoe

Housing The cloth covering a horse.

Huile (See **Goutty**)

Huitfoil (See **Octofoil**)

Human Heart (See **Heart**)

Humet (See **Hamade**)

Humetty (also **Humetté**) Couped at the ends, as of crosses, saltires and the like, the couped ends normally, but not invariably, following the contours of the shield. This term is derived from Humet. (see **Hamade**)

Saltire humetty

Hungerford knot (See **Knots**)

Hunting horn (See **Bugle horn**)

Hurst (also **Hurst of trees**) A clump of trees.

Hurt (also **Heurt**) Term applied to a roundel when it is blue.

Hurty (also **Hurté**) Semy of hurts.

Hydra A dragon with seven heads.

Ibex This is depicted like the heraldic antelope but the horns, usually serrated, point forwards rather than curve backwards.

Icicle The elongated gouttes bendwise in bend in the arms of Harbottle are sometimes blazoned icicles but it has also been suggested, and not without reason, that they may be hair bottles, that is leather bottles with the hair side outside.

Illegitimacy (See **Bastardy**)

Imbattled (See **Embattled** and **Partition, Lines of**)

Imbrued (See **Embrued**)

Impale To divide the shield per pale and place one coat on the dexter, another on the sinister side. A husband, when showing his marital coat, impales his wife's arms unless she is an heraldic heiress, in which case he places them on an escutcheon of pretence. Holders of certain offices, such as bishops and kings of arms, impale their personal arms with their official coat. When a bordure, orle, tressure, or charges in orle are impaled they are not continued down the palar line. The illustration shows the arms of John Balliol ('azure a lion rampant argent, crowned or') impaling those of Devorguilla his wife ('gules, an orle argent'). These are now the arms of Balliol College, Oxford.

Arms of
Balliol College

Imperial eagle The double-headed eagle is sometimes so called because of its use by the Holy Roman Emperors.

Imperial Service Order This award was instituted in 1902 and is now given to male and female members of the home, Commonwealth and Colonial Civil Service in recognition of faithful and meritorious service. Companions may add the letters ISO after their names and may suspend the badge beneath their shield of arms.

Impersonal arms (See **Arms of community**)

Incensed (also **Animé***) Spouting flames, particularly used in connection with panthers and other creatures having flames issuing from their ears and mouths.

Increment A moon in her increment is an increscent. (See **Crescent**)

Increscent A crescent whose horns face the dexter. (See **Crescent**)

Indented Notched like dancetty but with much smaller indentations (See **Partition, Lines of**)

Indian Empire, Order of the The Most Eminent Order of the Indian Empire was instituted in 1877. There are three classes, Knights Grand Commander, Knight Commander and Companion. All may suspend the badge of the order from their shield of arms and surround it with the circle and motto. Holders of the first class are entitled to a grant of supporters and may place the collar of the order round their arms. The order may be considered obsolescent, no appointments having been made to it since 1947.

Indivisible arms When a quartered coat has been granted by virtue of a Royal Licence it is termed an indivisible coat, for neither quartering may be borne singly, and if other quarterings are acquired the indivisible coat occupies one grand quartering, with the arms shown sub-quarterly; it is not divided to make two quarterings.

Indorsed (See **Addorsed**)

Inescutcheon When a shield or escutcheon is borne as a charge, especially where there is but one in the centre of the shield it is often so termed. (See **Escutcheon**)

Inflamed (See **Enflamed**)

Infulae The ribbons attached to the back of a mitre. They are also sometimes called 'labels'.

In glory Occasionally a synonym for 'irradiated'.

In lure Wings are said to be 'conjoined in lure' when joined at the base with tips pointing downwards, in the form of a hawk's lure.

Wings conjoined
in lure

In pretence The arms of a wife when an heiress are borne by her husband on an inescutcheon over his own coat. The arms are then said to be 'in pretence' or 'on an escutcheon of pretence', for the husband pretends to the headship of his wife's line.

Escutcheon
'in pretence'

Ingrailed A synonym for 'engrailed'. (See **Partition, Lines of**)

Ink moline (See **Mill rind**)

Insignia By insignia are meant the various badges of office, orders of knighthood and decorations which may be included in a full achievement of arms, although they are not strictly speaking part of the actual arms. The principal insignia used in connection with arms are as follows: the coronets of princes and peers; the mitres, ecclesiastical hats, episcopal crosses and croziers of ecclesiastics; the batons of field marshals, of the Earl Marshal and various other holders of high offices; the collars, ribands and badges of members of the orders of chivalry; the crowns of kings of arms and the collar of SS of kings and heralds of arms and others entitled to wear it; decorations, such as the VC, MC and GC but not campaign medals. It is important to note that a man's insignia, except for the coronets of peers, is personal and may not be used in connexion with marital arms. In such cases two shields are placed side by side, one showing the husband's arms alone with insignia, the other the marital coat without insignia. The two shields are ensigned by the helm, crest and mantling.

Interchanged (See **Counterchanged**)

Invected (See **Partition, Lines of**)

Inverted Reversed; turned upside down.

Involved (See **Encircled** and **Serpent**)

Irradiated (also **Radiated** and **In glory**) Surrounded by rays of light. An irradiated charge is usually shown as if it were charged on a sun.

Issuant Issuing or proceeding from. A chief with a demi lion rampant issuant means that the lion issues from the bottom line of the chief.

Jacent* Lying on its side.

Jall (See **Yale**)

Jamb (also **Gamb**) The lower part of a beast's leg, cut off at the second joint, unlike the paw which is cut off at the first joint.

Crest of lion's
jamb erased

Javelin Usually depicted as a short barbed spear.

Jelloped (also **Jowlopped***) A synonym for wattled, referring to the wattles of a cock who is frequently beaked, legged, combed (that is, crested) and jelloped or wattled of a different tincture from his body.

Jessant-de-lis A leopard's face jessant-de-lis is one that has a fleur-de-lis thrust through the mouth. This curious charge was anciently used by the Cantelupe family whose arms are now those of the see of Hereford. Sometimes the heads in this coat are shown ordinarily and sometimes reversed. It would seem that almost any animal's face can be shown in this way, there being a recent example of an ox's head jessant-de-lis.

Leopard's face
jessant-de-lis

Jess The short leather strap fitted to the legs of hawks and similar hunting birds. Most writers state that the bells are attached by the jesses but this is not so. The jess ends in a swivel or varvel through which the leash runs. The bells are attached by bewits. Birds of this sort are usually belled and also sometimes jessed.

Hawk's leg
belled
and jessed

Jewels There was once a fashion for using the names of jewels for the tinctures when blazoning the arms of noblemen. This conceit died a natural death but enjoyed a curious revival in the grant of arms made to the Gemmological Society of Great Britain in 1967. Topaz is used for or, pearl or chrystal for argent; gules, azure, sable, vert and purpure are respectively termed ruby, sapphire, diamond, emerald and amethyst; jacynth is used for tenné and sardonix for sanguine.

Jowlapped* (See **Jelloped**)

Jupiter Used for azure when blazoning by planets. (See **Planets**)

Jupon A short sleeveless coat, emblazoned with arms, which was worn over armour from c. 1350 to c. 1430. It succeeded the surcoat and was itself succeeded by the tabard.

Kaiser-i-Hind Medal   A decoration instituted in 1900 and several times amended. There are three classes, distinguished by gold, silver and bronze medals. It was awarded for the rendering of public service in India without distinction of race or sex. No awards have been made since 1947. A representation of the medal may be suspended beneath the shield.

Katherine wheel   (See **Catherine wheel**)

Key   When blazoning a key not only should its position in the shield be stated but also that of the wards.

King of Arms   Originally a king of heralds of arms. The senior rank of officer of arms. The crown of a king of arms is composed of sixteen acanthus leaves alternately high and low, set on a rim inscribed with the words *'Miserere mei Deus'*. (See **Crown** and Introduction, page 7).

Knight   Knights are either knights bachelor or knights of one of the orders of chivalry. All use in their arms a steel helm affronty with the visor raised. Knights of the orders of chivalry may also use the insignia appropriate to their degree. (See under the various orders of knighthood)

Knot   A variety of knots is known to armory. Often these knots are badges confined to a single family, like the Lacy knot. Others, which started as family badges, have become popular and are used as charges in arms. Such a one is the Stafford knot. Originally a badge of the Earls of Stafford it is now frequently, almost tediously, used in the municipal heraldry of Staffordshire. The illustrations depict the principal heraldic knots.

Bourchier knot   Bowen knot   Cavendish knot

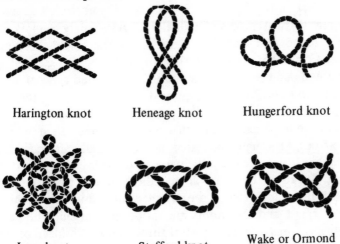

Harington knot   Heneage knot   Hungerford knot

Lacy knot   Stafford knot   Wake or Ormond knot

Kris A Malayan dagger or knife. There are various types of Kris but in heraldry a longish dagger with a wavy blade, broadening towards the hilt, is usually found. It has recently become a popular symbol of Malayan connections.

Label (also **File**) A horizontal band from which depend three vertical pieces. Originally it was solely a mark of difference and stretched right across the shield. As time went on the points, originally straight, became splayed at the ends and eventually a couped, dovetailed type of label was almost universally employed. Today, however, there is a welcome return to earlier practice. If a label has two or more than three points this must be mentioned in the blazon. Although the label is occasionally found as a charge, it is essentially the mark of difference for an eldest son. In royal heraldry all members of the royal family, both male and female, are assigned individual labels; these are argent and the points are variously charged. The heir-apparent has a label argent of three points. Children of the sovereign have labels of three and grandchildren of five points. The infulae of mitres are also sometimes called labels (See **Infulae**)

Three types
of label

Lacy knot (See **Knot**)

Lady Peeresses below the rank of duchess are frequently described as Lady So-and-so rather than by their full style. The daughters of dukes, marquesses and earls enjoy the honorary prefix of 'Lady' before their Christian names. Wives of Lords of Session in Scotland, baronets and knights are also accorded this style.

Lamb (See **Paschal Lamb**)

Lambrequin (See **Mantling**)

Lancaster Herald The title of one of the six heralds in ordinary. It has been so used since the reign of Henry VII, but previously Lancaster had been a herald to the Dukes of

Lancaster, the title first appearing in 1347. In the time of Henry IV Lancaster was king of the northern province and so remained until 1464 when Norroy became king of the province and Lancaster once again a herald's title. His badge is a red rose ensigned by the royal crown.

Latin cross (See **Cross**)

Langued Used to describe the tongue of a creature when of a different tincture from that of its body. Lions are understood to be armed and langued gules unless they themselves are red or are against a red background, in either of which cases the tongue and claws are shown azure.

Larmes (See **Goutty**)

Leaf A variety of leaves is found in heraldry. If the stalk is shown they are blazoned 'slipped' or 'stalked'.

Leg Human legs are usually shown as being flexed or embowed at the knee but it is best to specify this in the blazon. The triskeles of the Isle of Man are usually blazoned in full and not, as might be expected, by the one succinct term by which they are generally known. The rather tortuous blazon is: gules, three legs in armour proper, garnished and spurred or, flexed and conjoined in triangle at the upper part of the thigh.

Triskeles

Legged (See **Membered**)

Leopard In post-medieval blazon this term is properly applied only to the zoological beast. In early heraldry, what is now called the lion passant guardant was simply termed a leopard. Hence the expression 'the leopards of

England'.

Leopard's face   A leopard's head caboshed is so termed.

Letters   Letters of the alphabet occur occasionally in heraldry and the blazon should state whether a letter is a text (that is upper-case Old English text) or a Roman one (whether it is sans serif or not is immaterial).

Letters Patent   An open (Latin *patere* − to open) document addressed to everyone and with seal or seals pendent. Arms are granted by Letters Patent, the document being referred to as a Patent of Arms. The opposite of Letters Patent are Letters Close, which are addressed to one or more individuals and are closed with a seal.

Licence, Royal   (See **Royal Licence**)

Lily   This refers to the natural lily, in contradistinction to the fleur-de-lis, but even so it is usually drawn in a rather stylized way. The arms of Eton College contain three lilies.

Arms of
Eton College

Lined   When used of the mantling this term refers to the tincture with which it is lined, normally either a metal or a fur, although the more usual word is 'doubled'. The other sense in which it is used is when a line or leash is attached to a charge. Animals are frequently found 'collared and lined'.

Lines of partition   (See **Partition, Lines of**)

Lion   At once one of the oldest, most spectacular and most popular charges in armory. The lion is drawn in a variety of ways but seldom as seen in the zoo. Liberties are often taken with his anatomy, inasmuch as he frequently has but three claws on each paw, rather than the five on the fore-paws and four on the hind-paws with which nature has endowed him.

Lion rampant

Lion's face   A lion's head caboshed is so termed.

Lionced*   When the ends of a charge, such as a cross, terminate in lion's faces it may be so described.

Lioncel   When more than one lion appears on a shield the small lions were sometimes called lioncels, but this term is not now used.

Lion-dragon*   A monster having the foreparts of a lion and the hind-parts of a dragon.

Liver bird   The cormorant in the arms of the City of Liverpool is so blazoned but the name appears to be a purely local sobriquet.

Liveries   The livery colours were those in which a lord clothed his retainers and were frequently based on the principal colour and metal in the arms. From the beginning of the seventeenth century until recently crests were almost invariably granted 'on a wreath of the colours', meaning of the livery colours, which were deemed to be the first metal and colour mentioned in the blazon. (See **Wreath** and **Mantling**)

Lizard   The lucern or lynx was once termed a lizard, as in the grant of supporters and crest to the Skinners' Company of London in 1550. The natural lizard, sometimes termed a scaly lizard, is also to be found.

Lochaber axe   A type of bill, having a hook at the end

of a curved haft.

Lochaber axe

Lodged Used of animals of the deer variety when lying down. 'Harboured' is a synonym for lodged but is rarely used.

Stag lodged

Long cross (See **Cross**)

Lord Peers below the rank of duke are frequently described as Lord So-and-so rather than by their full style. The younger sons of dukes and marquesses enjoy the honorary prefix of Lord before their Christian names. Lords of Session in Scotland are also accorded this style.

Lotus flower This is sometimes shown in a stylized manner like the heraldic rose, as in the arms of Goonetilleke, and sometimes in perspective in its natural form, as in the arms of Jardine, baronet. No distinction is made in the blazon.

Lotus from arms
of Goonetilleke

Lotus from
arms of Jardine

Lozenge A charge shaped like a diamond in a pack of cards. If it is very long and narrow it is termed a 'fusil'. Spinsters and widows bear their arms on a lozenge rather than a shield and funeral hatchments are lozenge-shaped.

Lozengy Divided bendy and bendy sinister to give a pattern of lozenges.

Lozengy

Lucerne (See **Lizard**)

Lucy (also **Luce** and **Ged**) An old name for the pike but the one which is invariably used in armory.

Luna Used for argent when blazoning by planets. (See **Planets**)

Lure (See **Hawk's lure** and **In lure**)

Lymphad The heraldic galley. The blazon should state whether it is 'in full sail' or with 'sails furled'. If it is being rowed the term 'oars in action' is employed and it is also usual to state whether 'flags' and 'pennon' are flying.

Lymphad in
full sail

Lynx (See **Lizard**)

Lyon King of Arms The principal heraldic officer in Scotland. He is one of the five high officers of state and enjoys the style Right Honourable and the honorific prefix Lord. He alone exercizes the Crown's jurisdiction in matters armorial, conducts state ceremonies in Scotland and has jurisdiction in questions of name and change of name. Lyon is also a judge and presides over the Court of the Lord Lyon where rights to arms and pedigrees are established and where action is taken against those who infringe the Scottish laws of arms.

Mace Civic maces, symbols of authority, are sometimes used as charges. The spiked war mace is either termed a 'mace' or less equivocally a 'spiked mace' and was sometimes nicknamed 'holy water sprinkler'. It is also sometimes blazoned a 'mace of war', but as other miscellaneous varieties of war mace are also blazoned in this way the description is ambiguous.

Macle (See **Mascle**)

Maiden's head (See **Head**)

Maintenance, Cap of (See **Chapeau**)

Male griffin (See **Griffin**)

Mallet (also **Martel**) The ordinary wooden hammer is used; although various shapes are to be found the blazon does not normally refer to them.

Maltese Cross (See **Cross**)

Man antelope An heraldic antelope with a man's face. The supporters confirmed to Lord Stawell in 1682 are so blazoned but they are elsewhere referred to as 'satyrals'.

Manch (See **Maunche**)

Maned Used to describe the mane of a horse, unicorn, etc. (See **Crined**)

Man Lion A lion with a human face, the hair forming the mane.

Manticora (also **Mantiger**) This monster is found in various forms. Usually it has the body of an heraldic tyger, an old man's head with flowing beard and hair and two spiral horns. There are, however, examples (as in Lord Fitzwalter's badge) where the feet are human feet and there are no horns. The supporters of Lord Huntingdon's arms have no horns and are now depicted like man lions.

The Fitzwalter
manticora

Mantling (also **Lambrequin**) The short mantle fixed to and flowing from the helmet. Where a helmet is shown in an achievement of arms the mantling is an essential concomitant. Its origin is unknown but three theories are normally advanced to explain its existence: 1 that it helped to keep the sun off the back of the neck in hot climates; 2 that it was a piece of defensive armour, having the effect of deadening a sword blow on the neck; 3 that it was simply an attractive addition to a knight's accoutrements in the joust and tournament, having developed from the ribbons attached to early helms. Perhaps there is some truth in all three theories. A study of the early stall plates of the Knights of the Garter shows that the colour of the mantling was usually, although not invariably, the principal colour in the arms; it was not, however, lined with the principal metal. The mantling was sometimes patterned or strewn with one or more of the family badges. Under the early Tudor heralds the colours of the mantling were fairly capricious but in the second half of the sixteenth century the red and silver mantling became almost universal and remained *de rigueur* until the end of the eighteenth century. Thereafter the principal colour and metal in the arms were used for the mantling until quite recently, when there has been a return to early practice. Today the mantling may be of any tinctures, can be parted of two colours on the outside or two metals on the inside and can be spattered with the badge. A gold mantling doubled ermine is reserved for the Crown and royal princes and a mantling lined with ermine is granted only to peers.

Maple leaf The red maple leaf has recently been adopted as the principal Canadian emblem. This leaf was always an emblem of Canada, and as such frequently occurred in the arms of Canadian citizens and corporations, but now that it forms the principal charge on the Canadian flag, adopted in 1965, a single maple leaf is no longer granted.

Maple leaf

Marcassin* A young boar, distinguished from an old one by having a limp tail.

Marchioness The wife of a marquess or one who holds a marquisate in her own right.

Marine An old suffix which means the same as the present prefix 'sea' when describing certain monsters such as the sea-wolf, anciently wolf marine and so forth. (See **Sea-dog** and **Sea-monsters**)

Marks of cadency or difference (See **Difference, Marks of**)

Marquess (also **Marquis**) The second rank in the peerage. A continental title not introduced into England until 1385. (See **Peer**)

Mars Used for gules when blazoning by planets. (See **Planets**)

Marshal (See **Earl Marshal**)

Marshalling The art of correctly depicting a full achievement of arms with particular reference to the display of more than one coat on the shield. This is occasioned by marriage, inheritance or by holding an office to which arms pertain. (See **Impale, Quarter, Women's Arms** and Introduction page 16).

Martel (See **Mallet**)

Martlet A very common charge which resembles a house martin but has no shanks or legs, just tufts of feathers. It may originally have been a swift, as these apparently legless birds were to be found in large numbers in the Holy Land at the time of the Crusades. It is the mark of cadency for a fourth son.

Martlet

Mascle (also **Macle**) A voided lozenge. In 1788 John Christian was granted a 'demi-mascle'; the top half of the mascle, looking like a couped chevron, was depicted.

Mascle

Masculy Composed of conjoined mascles.

Mask (See **Fox's mask**)

Masoned When a charge is drawn so as to represent masonry it is so blazoned. If the lines of cement are of a different tincture from the charge (that is, not simply shaded in with a darker tone) the charge is said to be 'masoned of' the tincture of the cement.

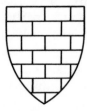

Shield masoned

Match This refers to the coiled fuse, not the modern safety match.

Matriculation By statute of the Scottish Parliament 1592, Chapter 125, and also by statute of 1672, Chapter 47, Scotsmen are forbidden to bear arms unless these have been properly matriculated, that is, marshalled by Lyon King of Arms with appropriate marks of difference. Only the heir male need not matriculate although even he is recommended to do so about every third generation. When arms are matriculated they are entered in the Public Register of All Arms and Bearings in Scotland.

Maunch (also **Manch** and **Maunche**) An ancient sleeve severed at the shoulder. The artist has a certain amount of licence in drawing this charge and two popular versions are here illustrated.

Two types
of maunch

Medals The insignia of orders of chivalry and decorations such as the Military Cross may be suspended beneath the shield, but not campaign nor commemorative medals.

Melusine A mermaid with two tails, although the only one known to English heraldry (in the arms of Vischer) is so blazoned and is not termed a melusine.

Membered Used to describe the legs of birds. The term 'legged' is also sometimes used.

Memorial The name given to the petition which a prospective grantee must address to the Earl Marshal asking for his Warrant to the kings of arms allowing them to grant.

Mercury Used for purpure when blazoning by planets. (See **Planets**)

Mercury, Rod of (See **Caduceus**)

Merit, Order of A very exclusive order which confers neither title nor precedence and has but one class. It was instituted in 1902 and the number of ordinary members is restricted to twenty-four. Members may suspend the insignia of the order beneath their arms.

Mermaid   The upper half of a young maiden with long hair conjoined to a fish's tail, which is usually bent round to the sinister. Mermaids are frequently depicted combing their hair with the sinister hand, whilst respecting themselves in a hand-mirror held in the dexter hand, but these accoutrements are not invariable and should be blazoned.

Mermaid with
mirror and comb

Merman   Usually called a 'triton' (q.v.).

Metals   The metals used in heraldry are gold (or) and silver (argent).

Midas's head   A man's head with long hair, a beard and the ears of an ass.

Military Cross   A decoration instituted in 1914 to reward distinguished and meritorious services rendered by those holding certain ranks in the army in time of war. A representation of it may be suspended beneath the shield.

Mill rind   (also **Mill iron, Fer-de-moline** or **Mouline** and **Ink moline**) The iron centrepiece of a millstone. It takes various similar forms, which are not distinguished in the blazon, and is normally shown palewise.

Three types
of mill rind

Mitre Mitres are used both as charges and as insignia of episcopal or abbatial dignity. Archbishops and bishops of the Anglican Communion ensign their arms with a mitre which, though often painted pale blue and white, would seem to represent the *mitra pretiosa* which pre-Reformation bishops and abbots (though probably incorrectly) used. Roman Catholic archbishops and bishops under the jurisdiction of the English kings of arms are entitled to ensign their arms with a *mitra pretiosa*, although a Papal Order in 1969 proscribed their use. Abbots may use the *mitra simplex*. This is a plain white mitre whereas the *mitra pretiosa* is of precious metal and is either jewelled or chased as jewelled. All mitres have infulae (ribbons) dependent from the back. The Bishop of Durham places his mitre within a ducal coronet as a symbol of the ancient palatinate or temporal jurisdiction enjoyed by the bishops. This jurisdiction was also sometimes symbolized by a plume of ostrich feathers issuing from the mitre.

Mitra preciosa

Mitra simplex

Mitry* Semy of mitres.

Mole This creature is generally associated with the heraldry of the Twistleton family. The blazon does not make it clear how the creatures should be shown but they are usually depicted as if flattened outward and seen from above.

Molet (See **Mullet**)

Monster Any fabulous creature is referred to, for purposes of classification, as a monster.

Moline   (See **Cross**)

Moon   The full moon is said to be 'in her complement' or 'in plenitude' and often has a human face to distinguish her from a plate. When the moon is not full she is a crescent and is so described unless a face is indicated. (See **Crescent**)

Moor's head   (See **Head**)

Morion   A steel cap, dating from the sixteenth century and sometimes used as a charge.

Morion

Mort's head*   A human skull or death's head.

Motto   The motto is either a war cry or other aphorism. Mottoes were first used in connection with the display of arms in the fourteenth and fifteenth centuries but were not in general use until the seventeenth century. The motto is usually written on a scroll, placed beneath the arms, although it is sometimes placed over the crest particularly if it is a war cry. A few families sport two mottoes, one above and another beneath the achievement. Mottoes are frequently depicted in grants of arms but seldom actually form part of the grant; thus many people use the same motto and often change their motto at will. Until recently women were denied mottoes but this has been altered and a woman may now augment her lozenge with a motto. In Scotland the position is different as mottoes are officially granted and, unless there are two, are normally borne over the crest. Women in Scotland may use mottoes.

Mound   (also **Orb**) The ball surmounted by a cross,

usually formy, which forms part of the regalia. It symbolizes temporal sovereignty beneath the cross of Christ. It surmounts the royal crown and the coronet of the heir-apparent.

Mound

Mount A grassy hillock. It often forms the base of a crest and a 'mount in base' is sometimes found in a shield. It occupies the whole of the base as in the illustration. A double mount has two humps and a triple mount three, the centre hump being elevated above the other two.

Oak tree on a
mount in base

Mullet (Also **Molet**) Originally the mullet was a spur rowel, from the French word *molette*, but it now has a stereotyped form and more often symbolizes a star than a spur rowel. Unless otherwise blazoned it has five points and is unpierced. If pierced the colour of the hole must be indicated, but if the field shows through there is no real need to state that it is 'pierced of the field' for it is reasonable to assume that this is the case. The aquatic mullet (*genus mullus*) is also found in heraldry but sufficiently infrequently to make the risk of confusion minimal.

Mullet

Mullet of six
points pierced

Mural crown (also **Mural coronet**) A crown in the form of an embattled wall. Three, five or even more battlements can be seen but the number is not normally mentioned in the blazon. It may ensign the arms of county councils, replace the wreath in the crests of boroughs and cities, and is granted to eminent soldiers. (See **Crown**)

Murrey A reddish-purple or mulberry colour. It is one of the stains and was a livery colour of Edward IV. It is often equated with 'sanguine' but today it is recognized as a separate and distinct colour. It has recently enjoyed, along with the other stains, a new popularity.

Musimon* The hybrid issue of a goat and a ram. It is said to have the body of a goat and the head of a ram but with both goat's and ram's horns.

Musion (See **Cat-a-mountain**)

Muzzled Used to describe a bear, dog or other beast when wearing a muzzle.

Nag's head Synonym for horse's head.

Naiant Swimming; used to describe fish swimming horizontally across the shield.

Naiant counter-naiant Fish naiant in alternate directions are so described.

Two lucies
counter-naiant

Nail The headless nail is usually depicted and is often blazoned a 'passion nail'.

Naissant Often confused with 'issuant' but properly applied to a charge issuing out of the middle of another charge, like a demi-lion naissant from a fess, as in the illustration.

Demi-lion
naissant
from a fess

Name and arms clause A clause in a will which requires the beneficiary to take steps to assume the name and arms of the testator, either in addition to or in lieu of his own, usually within a year of the testator's decease, as a requirement of inheritance. The way to comply with such a requirement is to petition the Crown for a Royal Licence to effect the change.

Naval crown (also **Naval coronet**) A crown which now consists of four hulks of ships alternating with four sails, although in the past the design has varied. It is granted to eminent sailors. (See **Crown**)

Navel point (See **Nombril point**)

Nebek A monster, similar to the heraldic tyger, but more hairy. It was the badge of Lord Fitzwilliam and is so named in any early sixteenth-century manuscript.

Nebuly (See **Partition, Lines of**)

Negro's head (See **Head**)

Neptune A triton or merman crowned and armed with a trident. (See **Triton** and **Trident**)

Neptune's horse (See **Sea-monsters**)

Nerved A synonym for veined when referring to the veins of a leaf.

Nimbus (See **Glory**)

Noble A much-abused and misunderstood word. In England it really refers only to peers who in their Letters Patent of creation are 'really ennobled' by the Crown. The lesser nobility are called gentry, as are those who are gentle in blood or by their calling. They are entitled to have arms although they do not necessarily possess them. A grant of arms recognizes gentility but does not create a nobleman. In Scotland, on the contrary, a grant of arms is in a sense a patent of nobility or what in England would be called gentility. On the continent the term 'noble' also has different connotations.

Nombril point (also **Navel point**) A point of the shield which is sited between the fess point and the base of the shield. (See **Points of the shield**)

Norroy King of Arms The junior of the two provincial English kings of arms. His jurisdiction used to lie north of the River Trent. The name Norroy has been consistently used for the northern king since 1464. In 1943 the office was joined to that of Ulster King of Arms so that Norroy and Ulster now has jurisdiction in the six counties as well as in the north of England. The arms of the office of

Norroy are: argent a cross gules, on a chief per pale azure and gules, a lion passant guardant, crowned with an open crown, between a fleur-de-lis and a key, all or. There are no arms for the combined office of Norroy and Ulster. (See **Ulster King of Arms**)

Nova Scotia, Baronets of (See **Baronet**)

Nowed Tied in a knot; frequently applied to serpents and the tails of beasts when knotted.

Serpent nowed

Nowy (See **Partition, Lines of**)
Nuclear symbols (See **Atomic heraldry**)

Oak   When an oak tree is blazoned 'fructed' a few large acorns should be depicted on its branches. Slips and branches of oak are of frequent occurrence.

Octofoil   (also **Eightfoil, Huitfoil** and **Double quatrefoil**) A flower like a cinquefoil but with eight petals. It is, somewhat illogically, the mark of difference for a ninth son.

Octofoil

Office, Arms of   (See **Arms of office**)

Officer of Arms   A generic term which comprehends pursuivants, heralds and kings of arms. There are thirteen officers of arms in ordinary who form the Corporation of the Kings, Heralds and Pursuivants of Arms, usually known as the College of Arms or Heralds' College. They are Garter, Clarenceux and Norroy and Ulster Kings of Arms; Chester, Windsor, Richmond, Somerset, York and Lancaster Heralds, and Portcullis, Bluemantle, Rouge Croix and Rouge Dragon Pursuivants. These officers are paid small salaries (a herald receives £17.16 *per annum*) by the Crown and are members of the Royal Household. Their activities are threefold. They are ceremonial officers, arranging state ceremonies under the Earl Marshal and taking part in them; they are the custodians and interpreters of the official heraldic and genealogical records, the kings of arms actually granting arms (see **Grant of arms**); and they conduct their own private practices as heraldic, genealogical and ceremonial consultants. From time to time the Crown creates officers of arms extraordinary. These are really honorary officers; they take part in the ceremonies of state but are not members of the College of

Arms and are not in receipt of any emoluments from the Crown. In Scotland the duties of the officers of arms are similar to those of the English officers, although in fact few of them run heraldic and genealogical practices. Apart from Lord Lyon King of Arms there are three heralds, Marchmont, Albany and Rothesay, and three pursuivantes, Carrick, Kintyre and Unicorn. There is no College of Arms in Scotland and since 1822 the officers of arms have received salaries, albeit unrealistic ones. Lyon is appointed by the Crown and himself appoints the other officers, both in ordinary and extraordinary.

Ogress (See **Pellet**)

Olive (See **Goutty**)

Ondé Undy. (See **Partition, Lines of**)

Opinicus In the grant of arms to the Plaisterers' Company of London this fabulous monster, two of which support the arms, is described as 'half serpent and half beste vert wynged membrid and eyed geules the throte and bely purfled golde'. It is depicted like a fat serpent with eagle's wings, a lion's legs, a long bill, pointed ears and an apology of a tail. Most textbooks show this monster with a lion's body, griffin's or dragon's neck and head, eagle's or dragon's wings and a camel's tail.

Opinicus

Oppressed (See **Debruised**)

Or The metal gold. It is frequently represented by yellow, a pale yellow ochre being favoured. It is indicated in engraving by small dots. It is sometimes but rather needlessly abbreviated *o*.

Orange   A roundel tenné may be so described, but in practice it is not, presumably to avoid confusion with the actual fruit, which is to be found as a charge.

Orb   (See **Mound**)

Order in Council   This is an Order made in the Privy Council. Under the terms of the Local Government Act 1972, which Act established new local authorities throughout England and Wales, provision was made for the arms of certain old authorities to be transferred to new authorities by an Order in Council rather than by a Royal Licence (q.v.). Broadly speaking, a new authority wishing to bear the arms of an old authority had to show that *pace* the new distribution of powers and authority detailed in the Act, it was virtually the same body as that which it superceded. This method of transferring arms is unique and must be regarded as *ad hoc* and not as setting a precedent.

Orders of chivalry or knighthood   These are detailed under the names of the various orders.

Ordinaries   Certain basic geometrical charges are, for convenience, termed ordinaries or honourable ordinaries. Unfortunately, whilst classification is often helpful, some confusion is caused by the inability of the writers of textbooks to agree as to what are and what are not honourable ordinaries. Most concede this distinction to the bend (and bend sinister), chevron, chief, cross, fess, pale, pile and saltire. Some writers reject the pile, whilst others include the bar and even the bordure and flaunches. The less honourable ordinaries are termed sub-ordinaries. Details of the ordinaries will be found under their various names.

Ordinary of Arms   A dictionary in which arms are listed alphabetically by the charges they contain, thus enabling a person proficient in blazon to identify arms. The best-known printed ordinary is A. W. Morant's edition of J. W. Papworth's *Ordinary of British Armorials,* published in 1874 and reprinted in 1961. There is also a number of pictorial and manuscript ordinaries of arms.

Oreiller* Synonym for a cushion.

Orle Like a bordure but not reaching the edges of the shield.

Orle

Orle, In Charges placed round the shield in the direction of an orle are said to be 'in orle'. An alternative blazon would be to describe them as an 'orle of' whatever the charges are. In ancient blazon the number of such charges would have been ignored but today it is usually stated.

Crescents in orle

Orthography The spelling of heraldic terms has always been capricious and it is true to say that even today different armorists will favour, nay almost fight and die for, certain spellings. The current tendency seems to be for anglicization of French words. Thus 'semée' is invariably spelled 'semy'. 'Dancettée' becomes 'dancetty', thus avoiding the problem of deciding whether it should always be masculine or feminine or agree with the noun it qualifies; in which case should the noun be given its French gender? Medievalists stick to the French form 'gardant' but most heralds ánd writers now use 'guardant'. The answer is that it does not really matter, but simple spellings are easiest to memorize.

Ostrich feathers in
badge of
Vickers Ltd.

Ostrich feather   This is usually shown with the end curled over. The quill or pen is often of a different tincture from the feather, which is then termed 'quilled' or 'penned' of that tincture.

Ounce   Only the blazon distinguishes between the ounce and the leopard.

Over all   (also **Surtout**) Used of a charge which is superimposed over several other charges. Frequently employed when blazoning an escutcheon of pretence.

Overt*   With open wings.

Owl   Unless otherwise blazoned the owl is shown as in the illustration. There is no rule but the heraldic owl most closely resembles the long-eared owl (*asio otus*).

Owl

Ox   Only the blazon normally distinguishes between the ox and the bull.

Padlock Various shapes of padlock are used as charges but the blazon does not always specify the type.

Pairle The French word for 'pall'. It has recently figured frequently in English blazon, as 'per pall' and is invariably blazoned 'tierce in pairle'. (See **Tierce**)

Pair of scales (See **Balance**)

Pale An ordinary consisting of a broad vertical band drawn down the centre of the shield. Normally the pale occupies about a third of the width of the shield but in the Canadian flag, approved in 1965, the pale occupies half the area of the flag and is blazoned 'a Canadian pale'.

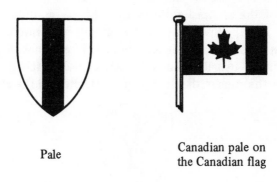

Pale

Canadian pale on the Canadian flag

Palewise Lying in the direction of the pale.

Palisado crown (also **Espallade crown**) A crown consisting of an indefinite number of pointed stakes fixed to a rim in the form of a palisade. (See **Crown**)

Pall A figure which, although of no great antiquity, is usually listed as a sub-ordinary and resembles the shape of the ecclesiastical vestment. The vestment itself, which occurs in the arms of the see of Canterbury and other ecclesiastical coats, is also sometimes blazoned 'a pall', which can lead to confusion. It is less ambiguous if the vestment is blazoned 'a pallium'. The pall granted to Thomas Sheriff, Rouge Dragon Pursuivant, in 1761 is curiously blazoned 'a cross pall'. (See **Shakefork**)

Pall

Pallet The diminutive of the pale. The term is not much used in modern blazon.

Pallium An ecclesiastical vestment which resembles the pall in shape but does not reach the bottom of the shield and is usually edged and fringed at the foot. In the arms of the archbishopric of East Africa, granted in 1962, there is a pallium but, although not mentioned in the blazon, the upper ends are couped, like a shakefork. The pallium is usually charged with crosses fitched, representing the pins with which it was attached to the chasuble.

Arms of the See
of Canterbury

Palmer's staff (also **Pilgrim's staff** and **Bourdon**) A staff ending in a knob which usually has a hook at the top from which a script, purse or wallet can be hung.

Palmer's staff

Paly Divided palewise into an even number of divisions, the number usually being specified. (See **Barry**)

Paly bendy Divided Paly and also bendy. Paly bendy sinister is divided paly and bendy sinister.

Paly bendy

Panache A fan or bank of feathers. Unless the blazon specifies otherwise these are shown as ostrich feathers and there are usually three rows.

Panes The pieces which form chequy and compony are sometimes so termed.

Panther The heraldic panther is now always shown incensed, that is with flames issuing from mouth and ears, although originally it lacked this attribute. It is also frequently spattered with roundels; the panther which supports the arms of the Duke of Beaufort is covered with blue, green and red spots.

Panther, the
dexter supporter
of the Duke of
Beaufort's arms

Parted Divided; a synonym for 'party'.

Partition, Lines of These are the lines which may be used to divide the shield or charges. When so divided the word 'per' precedes the name of the ordinary whose direction the line follows. Thus there is 'per fess', 'per pale', 'per chevron', 'per bend', 'per bend sinister' and 'per saltire'. 'Per cross' is usually termed 'quarterly', and 'per pall', 'tierced in pairle'. These lines and those with which certain geometrical charges are drawn are capable of a number of variations. The illustrations detail these, but as 'invected' and 'engrailed' can so easily be confused it should be noted that the points of the cups face outwards when engrailed and inwards when invected. When an ordinary is described as 'embattled' only the top edge is crenellated. If both edges are crenellated then it is blazoned 'embattled counter embattled' or, if the crenellations are opposite each other 'bretessed'.

Party (also **Parted**) Divided. This term sometimes precedes the word 'per' when a field or charge is divided. Thus 'per fess' may be rendered 'party (or parted) per fess' but really the word is superfluous, its principal use being to describe a mantling when parted of two colours or metals. Even here it is often omitted.

Paschal Lamb (also **Agnus Dei** and **Holy Lamb**) A lamb passant usually having a nimbus or halo behind the head, often charged with a cross formy throughout, and supporting with the dexter fore-leg a staff ending in a cross from which flows a white pennon charged with a red cross. Sometimes the lamb's accompaniments (halo, staff and flag) are blazoned separately, on other occasions 'paschal lamb' comprehends everything.

Pascuant* Grazing.

Passant Used to describe beasts who are walking along with the dexter fore-paw raised. (See **Counter** and **Trippant**)

Talbot passant

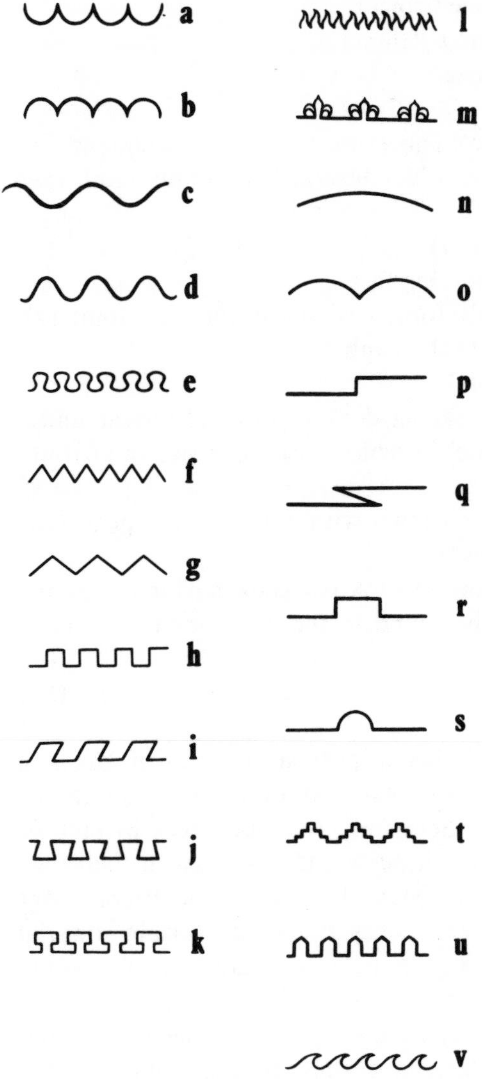

Lines of partition
a Engrailed
b Invected
c,d Wavy or Undy
e Nebuly
f Indented
g Dancetty
h Embattled or
    Battled
i Raguly
j Dovetailed
k Potenty
l Rayonné
m Flory or Fleury
n Arched or
    enarched
    or archy
o Double arched,
    enarched or archy
p Angled
q Bevilled
r Escartellé
s Nowy
t Embattled or
    battled, grady
u Urdy
v Crested

Passion cross   (See **Cross**)

Passion nail   (See **Nail**)

Pastoral staff   (See **Crozier**)

Patent   (See **Letters Patent**)

Patonce   (See **Cross**)

Patriarchal cross   (See **Cross**)

Paty   (also **Patée**) The cross formy was frequently so termed but today the older blazon is generally used. (See **Cross**)

Pavillion   (See **Tent**)

Pavon   A long tapering flag.

Paw   An animal's foot, cut off at the first joint and therefore shorter than the jamb.

Pawne*   A peacock.

Peacock   Shown facing dexter with tail closed unless blazoned 'in his pride' in which case he is shown affronty with tail displayed.

Pean   A black fur strewn with gold ermine spots. (See **Ermine** and **Tinctures**)

Pea-rise   (also **Pease-rise**) A pea-stalk having leaves and flowers. One is to be found in the crest of St Quintin of Harpham, Yorkshire.

Pearl   Used for argent when blazoning by jewels. (See **Jewels**)

Peer   One who holds a peerage in one of the five degrees, duke, marquess, earl, viscount or baron in the Peerage of England, Scotland, Ireland, Great Britain, or the United Kingdom. All peers and peeresses in their own right, except the Irish peers, may since the Peerage Act 1963 sit in the House of Lords. Peers have certain armorial privileges. They use a silver helm with gold bars facing the dexter, their coronet of rank ensigns their arms (see **Coronet**) and they may have supporters assigned to them, such supporters appertaining only to the holder of the dignity. It is generally held that a peer who disclaims his peerage under the terms of the 1963 Peerage Act renounces his armorial privileges. The two archbishops and the senior twenty-four diocesan bishops of the Established Church are know as spiritual peers and sit in the House of Lords. (See under the various titles)

Pegasus A winged horse. In classical mythology Pegasus was begotten by Poseidon and sprang forth from the bleeding body of Medusa, his mother, after she had been slain by Perseus.

Pelican This bird is nearly always shown with wings raised pecking her breast. In this position she is said to be 'vulning herself'. If shown standing on her nest with her young feeding on her blood she is blazoned 'a pelican in her piety'. Either way she is an ancient type of Christ, even though pelicans do not in fact shed their blood for their young.

Pelican
in her piety

Pellet (also **Gunstone** and **Ogress**) A black roundel.

Pellety Semy of pellets.

Pencil (also **Pencell, Pensell,** and **Pensil**) See **Pennoncelle**)

Pendent (also **Pendant**) Hanging down or dependent. The small forked pennon granted in the arms of Ricardo in 1814 is termed a 'pendent'.

Penned (See **Ostrich Feather**)

Penner and ink horn An ink bottle and a case for holding pens joined together by a cord.

Pennon A tapering lance flag, originally charged with arms but later with badges or crests.

Thirteenth-century
pennon (D'Aubernon)

Pennoncelle (also **Pencell**, **Pensell** and **Pinsil**) A tapering lance flag, similar to a pennon but shorter. In Scotland the pinsil is a triangular flag granted only to peers and feudal barons. It is four and a half feet long and bears the crest surmounted by coronet or chapeau within a circle inscribed with the title. In the fly the motto is shown on a scroll together with the plant badge, if there is one.

Per (See **Partition, Lines of** and **Party**)

Perclose The lower half of a garter, showing the buckle.

Petasus Originally a flat felt hat worn by the Thessalians. Hermes (Mercury) wore a winged petasus, so the term is now applied to a winged morion.

Petronal* A pistol.

Pheon An arrowhead with the barbs engrailed on the inner edge. It is borne with the point downward, unless otherwise blazoned. (See **Broad arrowhead**)

Pheon

Phoenix An imaginary bird, usually represented as a demi-eagle displayed issuing from flames. A more lively representation, and one which has appeared in several recent grants of arms, is that of the phoenix heads and phoenix in the arms and crest granted to the Painters' Company of London in 1486. Here the phoenix is a bird of many and brilliant colours with a long crest attached to the head.

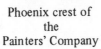

Phoenix crest of
the
Painters' Company

Pierced When a charge is so blazoned it implies that it is pierced through with a circular hole exposing the tincture of the field. If the hole is not circular the blazon should state the shape, and if some other tincture than that of the field shows through, this too must be specified. When a charge is pierced with an arrow (or similar weapon) then the arrow normally simply sticks into it and the expression 'vulned by' is sometimes used. If the arrow passes right through the charge then, although the term 'pierced' is sometimes used, 'transfixed' is a less ambiguous term.

Piety, in her (See **Pelican**)

Pike (See **Lucy**)

Pile An ordinary consisting of a triangular wedge issuing from the top of the shield. This charge is capable of various artistic representations. Originally a single pile was a long narrow wedge, the point almost touching the base of the shield. Later the top of the pile broadened and it grew shorter and shorter until some Victorian piles could easily have been blazoned 'per chevron reversed'. If more than one pile were shown, as in the arms of Sir Guy de Bryan (or three piles azure), these naturally came together in the base of the shield. However, when piles got shorter those whose points came together were blazoned 'in point' to differentiate them from those whose points were apart. Piles may issue from the sides of the shield or from the base. In the latter case they are sometimes termed 'transposed' or 'reversed'.

Pile
(post-medieval
design)

Three piles,
two in chief
and one in base

Pily Divided by conjoined piles throughout or almost throughout. This is sometimes blazoned 'pily counter pily'.

Pily bendy Like pily but with the divisions lying bendwise. 'Pily bendy sinister' implies that the piles go in the direction of bends sinister.

Pillar (See **Column**)

Pillow (See **Cushion**)

Pineapple This term is applied both to the fruit (*ananas sativus*), as in the arms of Jamaica, and to the cone of the pine tree. Something resembling the cone of the Scots pine is usually depicted.

Pineapples

Pinioned* Synonym for winged.

Piping shrike This bird, not unlike a magpie in appearance, was used to represent the state of South Australia in the arms granted to the Commonwealth in

1912. It is normally shown displayed and in this position, which it assumes rather uncomfortably, has been used in several coats granted to those having South Australian affinities.

Pizzled Used to describe the penis of an animal when of a different tincture from the body. (See **Sexed**)

Planets Just as there was once a passing fashion for giving the tinctures the names of jewels when blazoning the arms of noblemen, so was there a vogue for using the names of planets and other astral bodies for tinctures when blazoning the arms of princes. Even the astronomical signs were sometimes used as abbreviations. Sol was used for or, Luna for argent, Jupiter for azure, Mars for gules, Mercury for purpure, Saturn for sable and Venus for vert. The astronomical symbols are also occasionally used as charges.

The planets
a) Mars
b) Mercury
c) Jupiter
d) Saturn
e) Venus
f) Sol (sun)
g) Luna (moon)

Planta genista   The broom plant. A sprig of this plant showing leaves and open pods was a badge of the royal house of Plantagenet.

Planta genista

Plate   A term applied to a roundel when it is silver.

Platy   (also **Platté**) Semy of plates.

Plenitude   (See **Moon** and **Complement**)

Plume   Unless otherwise blazoned a plume of feathers is a bunch of about five ostrich feathers but usually the number and type of feather are specified in the blazon. Occasionally feathers banked up in rows are referred to as a plume but a panache (q.v.) is more usual.

Plumetty   (also **Plumette**) A design of overlapping feathers.

Plumetty

Point   This term is used of piles when their points meet but is otherwise almost entirely confined to the semi-mythical heraldry of abatements where various intrusions into the shield are known as points. Thus a point dexter parted tenné is said to be an abatement for a boaster. The unqualified term 'point' means the base of the shield (see **Base**)

Pointed (See **Cross**)

Points of the shield In order to facilitate the blazoning of arms the shield is divided into areas and certain points are named. The illustrations show the three points, honour (1), fess (2) and nombril (3), and also the various areas.

Points and areas
of a shield

Poix (See **Goutty**)

Pomegranate This fruit is shown with the skin split and the seeds showing through.

Pomegranate

Pomeis (also **Pomey** and **Pomme**) A term applied to a roundel when it is green.

Pommel The boss at the end of the hilt of a sword or dagger. (See **Hilt** and **Cross**)

Popinjay A parrot. If blazoned 'proper' it is shown as being green with red beak and legs.

Port A gateway or doorway, usually of a castle.

Portcullis The heraldic representation usually shows about four horizontal and four vertical bars with points at the bottom. Normally chains ending in rings are attached to the top corners but even so it is usual to blazon a portcullis as 'chained' if the chains are present. The portcullis was a Beaufort badge which was adopted by King Henry VII, whose mother was Margaret Beaufort. A crowned portcullis is still the royal badge used in connection with the Palace of Westminster and often signifies connections either with Parliament or with the City of Westminster. Uncrowned it is the badge of Portcullis Pursuivant and, ensigned with the royal crown, of Somerset Herald.

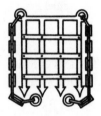

Portcullis
chained

Portcullis Pursuivant The title of one of the four pursuivants in ordinary, instituted by King Henry VII. The name alludes to the portcullis badge of the Beauforts, which was much used by Henry himself. A chained portcullis is the badge of this pursuivant.

Potent This was an ancient name for a crutch. Thus the cross potent (see **Cross**) has crutched ends. The name is also given to a supposed fur which is really hair with the cups drawn like crutch ends. This bogus fur has scarcely ever been used; still less has potent counter potent, sometimes termed 'tass', or 'tassy vairy'. (see **Cuppa**)

Potent   Potent counter potent

Potenty   (See **Partition, Lines of**)
Poudré*   (also **Powdered**) (See **Semy**)
Prefect Apostolic   (See **Protonotary Apostolic**)
Pretence, Escutcheon of   (See **Escutcheon**)
Pretension, Arms of   (See **Arms of Pretension**)
Preying   An animal eating his prey is said to be 'preying upon it'; in the case of birds the word 'trussing' is sometimes used.

Pride, Peacock in his   (See **Peacock**)
Priest   A Roman Catholic priest ensigns his arms with a black ecclesiastical hat with one tassel on either side. Some high church Anglican clergymen have followed this usage.

Privy Chamberlain to the Pope   Privy chamberlains and privy chaplains to the Pope both ensign their arms with a black ecclesiastical hat having six violet tassels pendent on either side.

Proboscis   The trunk of an elephant.

Pronunciation   Many heraldic terms can properly be pronounced in more than one way. For example pursuivant is usually pronounced 'persevant' but to pronounce it as spelt is not wrong. Gules can be 'jules' or the 'g' can be hard. The latter is the more usual pronunciation but the former is not incorrect. Words derived from the French are invariably pronounced as if they were English. Thus vert is not 'vaire' but is pronounced as written, as are all words ending in '-ant', like rampant, passant, volant, etc. It is best, therefore, to pronounce the terms of armory as they are spelt, for if this is done there are few chances of falling into error.

Proper When a charge is shown in its natural colour it is so termed. In theory a charge which is proper may lie on either colour or metal but the kings of arms, quite rightly, employ rule of eye as well as rule of thumb. It is abbreviated *ppr.*

Protonotary Apostolic A protonotary, vicar or prefect apostolic ensigns his arms with a crimson ecclesiastical hat having six tassels pendent on either side. Honorary or titular protonotaries apostolic use the same hat but it is black not crimson.

Provincial Kings of Arms Kings of arms who have jurisdiction over a province. In England there are two provinces, north of the river Trent, ruled by Norroy King of Arms, and south, ruled by Clarenceux King of Arms. In 1943 Norroy was given jurisdiction in Ulster and is now called Norroy and Ulster King of Arms.

Purfled Used as a synonym for 'garnished' but more often applied to the ornamentation of materials, such as sleeves, rather than of metal objects. (See **Garnished**)

Purpure The colour purple. It is usually shown as mauve rather than a deep purple. In engraving, diagonal lines in bend sinister are used to indicate purpure. It is abbreviated *purp.*

Pursuivant of Arms The junior rank of herald. (See **Officers of Arms**)

Python The heraldic python is a winged serpent, more like that slain by Apollo than the genus of giant snakes of that name. The monster granted to Isaac Teale in 1723 is clearly blazoned 'a python' but equally clearly it is nothing more nor less than a wyvern (q.v.).

Cross forming quadrate

Quadrate When a rectangle is shown in the centre of any form of cross it is blazoned 'quadrate'.

Quarter A sub-ordinary (sometimes classified as an ordinary) which occupies one quarter of the shield. Unless otherwise mentioned it is always the dexter chief quarter, being really no more than an enlarged canton. When a shield is divided into four 'per cross', then the divisions are called quarters.

Quarterly Literally 'divided per cross', but a shield divided into rectangular divisions by lines palewise and fesswise is described as quarterly of as many pieces as are formed by the dividing lines, unless of course the pieces are so small as to be chequers.

Quarterings The usual method of displaying arms inherited through heiresses is to divide the shield quarterly and place one coat in each quarter. The quarterings are numbered from dexter chief reading across like a book. The family arms are placed in the first quarter, then the inherited arms in order of acquisition. If there are insufficient quarterings to fill a symmetrically divided shield, for instance if there are seven, then the shield is divided into eight quarters, the arms in the first quarter being repeated in the last. Frequently a person is entitled to or only wishes to display one quartering in addition to the family arms. In this case the shield is divided into four, the family arms being placed in the first and fourth and inherited quartering in the second and third quarters.

Whilst today, and since Tudor times, quarterings have been inherited from uterine ancestors who are heraldic heiresses, in feudal days arms were often associated with lordships, and schemes of quarterings usually illustrated inheritance of property rather than blood, although of course the blood was usually present. A classic example is afforded by the arms of Richard Neville, Earl of Warwick and Salisbury, the 'King Maker', as displayed on an equestrian seal. Here Monthermer and Montagu are quartered on the front of the horse trapper, whilst on the back Beauchamp quarters the arms of the old Earls of Warwick, and Clare quarters Despenser.

Sometimes a quartering is itself quartered to show two or more coats. This method of marshalling, once used in England and still used in Scotland, is known as sub-quarterly or counter-quarterly. In such cases the main quartering is sometimes referred to as a grand quartering so as to avoid confusion. Today the only case where a quarter is counter-quartered is when an indivisible quartered coat, granted by Royal Licence, has to be marshalled in a scheme of quarterings.

Whilst quarterings are of historical interest, it is often impracticable to display more than four. A person is at liberty to select which quarterings he uses but he must never omit to show how they were acquired. For example if a man's grandmother were an heiress of Brown and in the right of her mother were entitled to display de Vere, her grandson could not elect to show de Vere without also displaying Brown, because he would never have inherited the noble arms of de Vere as a quartering had it not been conveyed to him by the more humble Browns.

Quarterly shield

Method of arranging
seven quarterings

Quatrefoil A four-leaved figure which, like the cinque-foil, can be pierced and is occasionally found 'slipped' like the trefoil.

Quatrefoil

Queen The title given to the consort of the king or to the ˙reigning monarch when a woman. A queen regnant bears the royal arms in the same way as the king, for the office or estate of queen, like that of any other corporate body, is deemed to be masculine. It has been customary for queens consort to bear the royal arms impaling their family arms, surmounted by a royal crown, the whole supported by the dexter royal supporter and their paternal sinister supporter.

Queue The tail of an animal.

Queued Tailed. (See also **Double-queued**)

Queue fourchy This is a forked tail and should not be confused with 'double-queued'. The latter expression indicates two separate tails emerging from the base of the spine; the former means a tail which divides about a quarter of the way up.

Lion rampant
queue fourchy

Lion rampant
double-queued

Quilled (See **Ostrich feather**)

Quise, à la (also à la cuise) When a bird's leg is cut off at the thigh (French – *cuisse*) it is said to be 'erased' (or 'couped' as the case may be) 'à la quise'.

Eagle's leg
erased a la quise

Rabbit Invariably blazoned 'coney'.

Radiated (See **Irradiated**)

Ragged staff The famous Warwick badge. It is a staff with the branches roughly hewn off.

Raguly (See **Partition, Lines of**)

Rainbow This is normally depicted as a semi-circle, each end issuing from clouds. Although these clouds are not always mentioned in the blazon it is safer to refer to them as there are examples of cloudless rainbows.

Raised in benediction (See **Benediction**)

Rampant The commonest position adopted by heraldic beasts. The left hind-leg is shown on the ground whilst the other legs wave fiercely in the air. The whole beast, unless otherwise blazoned, faces the dexter.

Raven This bird is sometimes so blazoned but is also called a corbie.

Rayonné (See **Partition, Lines of**)

Rebated* Broken off or cut short.

Rebus A picture which represents a word, as in canting arms. The term rebus, however, has been more or less reserved for non-heraldic badges which pun on the name of the bearer. Thus, Thomas Goldstone, Prior of Christ Church, Canterbury, used the rebus of a golden flint-stone ensigned by a mitre.

Recercelée (See **Cross**)

Red Ensign (See **Ensign**)

Reflexed (also **Reflected**) Curved backwards; usually applied to a chain when attached to a creature's collar and then 'reflexed' over the back'.

Regarding (See **Respectant**)

Lion rampant
reguardant

Reguardant (also **Regardant**) In early blazon this term usually signified what today we call guardant but it now means looking back over the shoulder.

Religious superior Roman Catholic religious superiors, both general and provincial, ensign their arms with a black ecclesiastical hat having six tassels pendent on either side.

Removed* Said of an ordinary when not in its usual position.

Renversé (See **Reversed**)

Replenished Filled with; also a rarely used synonym for 'semy'.

Reremouse (also **Rearmouse**) Old English word, still used in some dialects and in heraldry, for a bat.

Respectant (also **Aspectant, Encoutrant, Respecting** or **Regarding**) Used to describe two creatures facing each other. If the animals are rampant respectant then the single word 'combattant' is usually employed.

Rest (See **Clarion**)

Reversed (also **Renversé** and **Subverted**) Turned upside down. For example, a chevron reversed emanates from the chief and points towards the base.

Chevron reversed

Reynard* A fox.

Riband (also **Ribbon**) A diminutive of the bend, being even narrower than the bendlet. Actual strips of ribbon are also found in heraldry, as are the ribands of the various orders of chivalry.

Richmond Herald The title of one of the six heralds in ordinary. Originally a private herald belonging to the holders of the Honour of Richmond in Yorkshire. Since Henry, Earl of Richmond, came to the throne as King Henry VII in 1485, Richmond has been the title of a royal officer of arms. His badge is a red rose dimidiated with a white rose en soleil barbed and seeded proper ensigned by the royal crown.

Ringed This generally refers to the ring at the end of a chain or cord.

Rising (also **Rousant**) A bird about to take flight with wings open is so described.

Rock Rocks often occur in the base of a shield or as part of a crest. A rock is normally shown as a rugged mound and if blazoned 'proper' is shown grey.

Rod of Aesculapius (See **Aesculapius, Rod of**)

Rolls of arms Manuscript rolls or books listing, either pictorially or in blazon, armorial bearings. Old rolls of arms provide valuable evidence for the early development and use of armory. A valuable catalogue of these rolls has been compiled by Mr (now Sir) A.R. Wagner, entitled *Aspilogia I—A Catalogue of English Medieval Rolls of Arms* (Society of Antiquaries, 1950).

Rompu Broken. A chevron rompu is broken in the middle. Per bend rompu is the curious division of the shield in the arms of Allen of Suffolk. Any charge which is broken may be described as 'rompu'.

Per bend
sinister rompu

Chevron rompu

Rook This should refer to the bird but is sometimes and confusingly used as an abbreviation for the chess rook, as in the arms granted to Robert Walter in 1603.

Rose The heraldic rose is a five-petalled rose of the common sweet briar or dogrose variety. The sepals show between the petals and the centre of seeds, as in the natural rose, is large. When a rose is blazoned 'barbed and seeded proper', the barbs or sepals are shown green and the seeds gold. Artists sometimes superimpose an inner set of five petals. This is incorrect and probably originates in mistaking the Tudor rose for the ordinary rose. The Tudor rose consists of a white rose superimposed on a red rose barbed and seeded proper and was a badge much favoured by the Tudors as symbolizing the union of the two houses of York and Lancaster, brought about by the marriage of Henry VII to Elizabeth of York. Occasionally a Tudor rose composed of a red rose on a white one is depicted, as in the decoration on the earliest extant Garter of the Order of the Garter, now preserved at Anglesey Abbey, Cambridgeshire. If a rose is shown with a stem and leaves, as in the arms of Cope, baronet, then it must be blazoned 'slipped and leaved'. Sometimes such a rose is shown as a cultivated garden rose, but unless it is of a named genus the blazon makes no distinction between the two. A rose is the mark of a seventh son.

Rose   Tudor rose

Rose en soleil   A rose charged upon a sun. A white rose en soleil was a noted Yorkist badge and, ensigned by the royal crown, is now the badge of York Herald.

Rose en soleil

Rouge Croix Pursuivant   The title of one of the four pursuivants in ordinary. Mention of this title, which derives from the red cross of St George, is first found in the reign of King Henry V. His badge is a red cross couped.

Rouge Dragon Pursuivant   The title of one of the four pursuivants in ordinary. This office was created by King Henry VII on the eve of his coronation in 1485. The title refers to the royal Tudor badge of a dragon, the 'red dragon of Cadwallader', and Rouge Dragon's badge is a red dragon passant on a green mount.

Roundel   A disc, the name of which varies according to its tincture. If gold, it is a bezant; if silver, a plate; if red, a torteau; if blue, a hurt; if vert, a pomeis, pomey or pomme; if black, a pellet, ogress or gunstone; if purple, a golpe; and if barry wavy argent and azure, a fountain. Sometimes a roundel tenné is called an orange, and a roundel sanguine, a guze. It is sometimes said that bezants, plates and fountains should always be depicted as flat discs, whilst other roundels may be shaded to indicate that they are spherical, but ancient examples do not lend substance to this theory. It should be remembered that in medieval blazon (i.e. before the late fifteenth century) the terms bezant, pellet, torteau and some others were used freely to describe roundels more or less irrespective of the tincture, which was always mentioned.

Rousant (See **Rising**)

Rowel (See **Spur**)

Royal Air Force ensign (See **Ensign**)

Royal arms The royal arms as borne by the monarch are arms of sovereignty or dominion rather than family arms. Cadets of the royal house bear the royal arms as family arms but with marks of difference assigned to them by the sovereign. Normally sons and daughters of the sovereign receive labels of three points, and grandchildren labels of five points, variously charged. These labels are placed on the arms, crest and supporters. Royal heraldry is a law unto itself, although certain conventions are usually observed, for the fount of honour cannot be curbed in such a personal and virtually non-constitutional matter as the bearing of arms.

Royal Licence A special licence from the Crown which sets aside the normal laws of heraldry or honour in a particular instance. Such licences are addressed to the Earl Marshal and they must be recorded in the College of Arms before they become effective. They are signed by the sovereign and the Secretary of State for Home Affairs, who advises the Crown in matters of this nature. Royal Licences are frequently granted in cases where someone wishes to assume the arms of another, usually because of a testamentary injunction or when a bastard or adopted child wishes to be granted his father's arms. They are also granted to the brethren of peers who have no courtesy title, their father not having lived to inherit the peerage, to give them the precedence they would have enjoyed had their father lived to succeed. (See also **Order in Council**)

Royal Red Cross, Order of the This order was instituted in 1883 and is awarded to royal ladies and members of officially recognized nursing services in recognition of competency and devotion in nursing the sick and wounded of the armed forces. There are two classes, Members (RRC) and Associates (ARRC) and they may suspend the badge beneath their arms.

Royal Standard The banner of the royal arms is invariably, even in some official pronouncements, referred to as the 'royal standard' although it is manifestly technically not a standard (see **Banner** and **Standard**). The flying of this flag is the sole prerogative of the sovereign and it should not be flown by any subject of the crown, however loyal.

Royal Victorian Chain (See **Victorian Chain, Royal**)

Royal Victorian Order (See **Victorian Order, Royal**)

Ruby Used for gules when blazoning by jewels. (See **Jewels**)

Rudder This sometimes occurs as a charge and is usually depicted as in the illustration.

Rudder

Rustre A lozenge round-pierced. It is religiously referred to in all the textbooks but does not yet seem to have made its appearance in official armory.

Rustre

Sable   The colour black. It is usually a slightly greyish shade. In engraving cross-hatching (see **Hatching**) indicates sable. It is abbreviated *sa.* or *s.*

Sagittarius   (also **Sagittary**) A centaur with bow and arrow.

St Andrew's cross   A silver saltire on a blue field, being the Scottish national flag, is so termed.

St Anthony's cross   (See **Cross**)

St George's cross   A cross gules on an argent field, being the national flag of England, is so termed. Any charge described as being 'of St George', such as 'a canton of St George', is argent with a red cross throughout.

St John of Jerusalem, Most Venerable Order of   Usually called the Order of St John, but correctly the Grand Priory in the British Realm of the Most Venerable Order of St John of Jerusalem. This order is a charitable body having similar ideals to the ancient Order of St John now popularly known as the Order of Malta. It received a Royal Charter in 1888 when Queen Victoria became Sovereign Head of the order. Membership confers no precedence nor title but members of all grades may suspend their ribands and badges from their armorial bearings. The grades are as follows: 1 Bailiff and Dame Grand Cross, 2 Knight and Dame of Justice and Grace, 3 Commander (Brother and Sister), 4 Officer (Brother and Sister) 5 Serving Brother and Sister and 6 Esquire. Members of the first grade are entitled to a grant of supporters and may bear the arms of the order (gules, a cross argent, in the first quarter a representation of the sovereign's crest proper) as a chief to their arms. Members of the second grade, which includes chaplains, may bear their arms on the badge of the order (a white Maltese cross embellished in the four angles alternately with a lion passant guardant and an unicorn passant). The headquarters and chapel of the order are at St John's Gate, Clerkenwell.

St Julian's cross   A cross crosslet (see **Cross**) placed saltirewise.

St Michael and St George, Order of The Most Distinguished Order of St Michael and St George was instituted in 1818 and has subsequently been enlarged and extended on no less than fifteen occasions. There are three classes, all of which are limited: 1 Knight and Dame Grand Cross, 2 Knight and Dame Commander and 3 Companion. All classes suspend the appropriate insignia beneath their arms and surround their shield with the circle and motto of the order. Holders of the first class are entitled to a grant of supporters and may place the collar of the order round their arms. The order has its own king of arms and its chapel is in the south aisle of St Paul's Cathedral.

St Patrick's cross A saltire gules on a field argent, being the old national flag of all Ireland, is so termed.

St Patrick, Order of The Most Illustrious Order of St Patrick was instituted in 1783, revised in 1905, and may now be considered obsolescent, no appointments having been made since 1934. It consists of the sovereign and twenty-two knights. These are entitled to a grant of supporters, to encircle their arms with the collar, circle and motto of the order and to suspend the badge beneath the arms. Norroy and Ulster King of Arms is the Registrar and Knight Attendant and the banners and stall plates of the knights are still in St Patrick's Cathedral, Dublin.

St Stephen's cross A cross moline. (See **Cross**)

St Thomas's cross A plain cross couped charged with an escallop.

Salamander

Salamander A reptile which is supposed to live in fire. It is generally shown as a lizard surrounded by flames but early examples show it as a wingless dragon among flames (as such it was borne as a badge by Francis I of France, who died in 1547). In the garter stall plate of James, ninth Earl of Douglas. who died in 1488, the salamander looks more like a dog breathing flames.

Salient Used to describe beasts when springing or leaping. The term 'springing' is usually used when describing beasts of the deer kind when shown in this position, and 'forcene' is used of horses.

Tyger salient

Saltire An ordinary consisting of a cross placed diagonally on the shield. Charges on a saltire are normally placed erect but sometimes, without it being mentioned in the blazon, saltirewise. The lozenges in most Dalrymple coats are so depicted.

Saltire

Saltirewise (also **Saltireways**) Assuming the direction of a saltire; 'in saltire' means the same thing.

Saltorel* A diminutive of the saltire.

Sang (See **Goutty**)

Sangliant Embrued or stained with blood.

Sanguine Blood-red or crimson colour. It is one of the stains, and although often equated with murrey it is recognized today as a distinct colour and, with the other stains, has recently become popular.

Sans Means 'without' and is chiefly used to describe a creature who is missing a limb or part, such as a 'lion sans tail' or a 'dragon sans wings'.

Sans Nombre Literally numberless, but used as an alternative to 'geratting'. Both terms are unnecessary but if one were to be preferred 'sans nombre' has the edge over 'geratting' as the latter is a noun. In fact 'semy' is deemed sufficient to describe a field strewn with many small charges. Whether or not they are cut off by the outline of the shield is generally considered a matter for the artist to decide.

Sapphire Used for azure when blazoning by jewels. (See **Jewels**)

Saracen's head (See **Head**)

Sardony Used for sanguine when blazoning by jewels. (See **Jewels**)

Saturn Used for sable when blazoning by planets. (See **Planets**)

Satyr The half-man, half-goat of mythology is depicted in its normal (or perhaps abnormal) way in heraldry.

Satyral A monster having an old man's face, lion's body and antelope's tail and horns. It more closely resembles the manticore than the satyr of Greek mythology. (See **Man Antelope**)

Savage, dexter
supporter of
the Duke of
Edinburgh's arms

Savage A wild man and often so described. He is usually long-haired, bearded, wreathed about temples and loins with leaves and carrying a club.

Saxon crown A crown consisting of four (three visible) bifurcated uprights on which rests a ball. (See **Crown**)

Scales, Pair of, (See **Balance**)

Scaling ladder A ladder with hooks at one end to secure it to the top of the obstacle to be scaled. Such ladders feature largely in the heraldry of the Lloyds of West Wales descended from Cadifor ap Dinaval. A scaling ladder, now usually shown with three vertical supports, is the crest of the Northumberland family of Grey.

Scaling ladder

Scarpe* A diminutive of the bend sinister. 'Bendlet sinister' is the term in common use.

Sceptre When this emblem of sovereignty is borne as a charge it is normally shown as an ornamental rod rather than one of the two sceptres that form part of the regalia.

Scimitar (also **Scimetar** and **Scymetar**) A broad-bladed, curved sword, sometimes engrailed on the back edge. (See **Falchion** and **Seax**)

Scorpion

Scorpion Shown erect and in a somewhat stylized manner.

Scotland When the expression 'of Scotland' is used in a blazon it means 'of the royal arms of Scotland' (i.e. or, a lion rampant within a double tressure flory-counterflory gules). Whilst on the Great Seal of the United Kingdom the royal arms are shown with England in the first and fourth quarters and Scotland in the second, on the Great Seal for use in Scotland these quarterings are reversed and the Scottish supporters, crest and motto are used.

Scotland, Bordure of The double tressure flory counterflory gules.

Script (also **Scrip**) A palmer's wallet, purse or pouch. It can be borne pendent from a palmer's staff or else as a separate charge. It is usually blazoned a 'palmer's script'.

Scroll (See **Escroll**)

Scotcheon (also **Scutcheon**) (See **Escutcheon**)

Sea, Waves of When a blazon refers to 'waves of the sea proper' sometimes the conventional barry wavy argent and azure is shown and sometimes a realistic sea.

Sea-dog A talbot with webbed feet, scales, a dorsal fin and a rudder like an otter's. It used to be blazoned a 'hound marine' but this term is no longer used.

Sea-dog

Sea-monsters A sea-monster, which is a term of convenience, not a technical term, is created by joining the top half of a beast or monster to the tail of a fish, the sea-dog and 'sea-wolf being exceptions. Sometimes, though the practice is capricious, a continuous dorsal fin and webbed forefeet are shown. Common sea-monsters are sea-horses, -lions, -dragons, -unicorns, -bulls, and -stags but new ones are sometimes invented, often with wings added (see **Winged**).

At one time such creatures were frequently blazoned by their name followed by the term 'marine' but this fashion no longer pertains. The natural sea-lion and sea-calf are not distinguished in blazon from the monstrous hybrids, but the aquatic sea-horse, also called Neptune's horse, is invariably blazoned a 'sea-horse (hippocampus)'.

Sea-bull

Sea-wolf This is depicted without a fish's tail in much the same manner as a sea-dog. It used to be called a 'wolf marine'.

Seax A broad-bladed, curved sword like a scimitar but with a semi-circular notch in the back. A Saxon sword, it occurs in the arms of the counties of Essex and Middlesex and in those of many places and people associated with the ancient kingdoms of the East and Middle Saxons. (See **Scimitar** and **Falchion**)

Three seaxes

Seeded   This refers to the seeds of a flower and most frequently to those of the rose.

Segreant   Used as a synonym for 'rampant' when describing a griffin in this posture.

Sejant   (also **Sejeant**) Used to describe beasts in the sitting position with forepaws on the ground and facing the dexter. Variations in the position of forepaws, body or head must be noted, such as the lion in the illustration, which is sejant guardant.

Lion sejant
guardant

Semy   (also **Semé, Aspersed, Replenished, Strewed, Strewn, Poudré** or **Powdered**) Strewn or powdered with small charges. Some armorists distinguish between a field strewn with charges which are cut off by the outline of the shield or other charges (semy) and those where none is so shown (sans nombre and geratting), but such distinctions have seldom if ever been made and do not pertain today. Special terms are used for certain forms of semy: thus when a field or charge is semy of bezants it is blazoned 'bezanty'; of billets 'billety'; of cross crosslets (fitchy) 'cruisiey (fitchy)'; of fleurs-de-lis 'semy-de-lis'; of gouttes 'goutty' and of plates 'platy' (See under the various names)

Semy-de-lis

Serpent These are usually found nowed or encircled, but they may assume other positions such as erect and glissant. They are frequently found entwined about other charges such as in the rod of Aesculapius and about the necks of the three childrens' heads in the arms borne by the descendants of Moreiddig Warwyn.

Sexed Used to describe the genitals of an animal when of a different tincture from the body. The terms 'coded' and 'pizzled' (q.v.) are also found.

Shackbolt (also **Shackle Bolt**) A manacle or handcuff.

Shackbolt

Shafted Used when referring to the shaft of a spear, arrow or similar weapon.

Shakefork A charge similar to a pall but couped and with each of the three ends pointed. It is the basic charge in the armory of the Scottish family of Cunninghame (also Conyngham, Cunningham, etc.). Sometimes, but rarely, it is called a hayfork.

Shakefork

Shamrock This is drawn like a trefoil slipped but with broader, scalloped leaves. Not surprisingly it occurs in the arms of Irish families and families of Irish extraction and is blazoned as a shamrock. If it has four leaves, as that in the crest of Hart, baronets of Kilmoriarty, Co. Armagh, this must be mentioned.

Shank The upright part of an anchor. Also termed the beam. (See **Anchor**)

Sheaf Used to describe a bundle of arrows. (See **Garb**)

Sheldrake (See **Shoveller**)

Shield The principal vehicle for the display of the actual arms. This is one of the marks which distinguishes heraldry from other forms of symbolism. There are no rules as to what shape of shield shall be used in any given armorial display; the blazon of the arms, the nature of the display, the skill and knowledge of the artist and the aesthetic canons of the day generally combine to produce a finished design. After shields were no longer used, many fanciful often unrepentantly rococo shields were invented and characterize much of the heraldry of the eighteenth and nineteenth centuries. An interesting post-war innovation is the introduction of the African war-shield as a vehicle for depicting the arms of some of the new African states. Tanganyika was the first country to be granted arms on such a shield in 1961. The illustrations show a small selection of shields both possible and impossible, which have been used in heraldry.

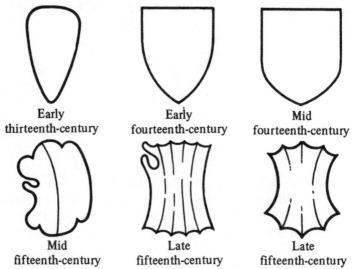

Early thirteenth-century   Early fourteenth-century   Mid fourteenth-century

Mid fifteenth-century   Late fifteenth-century   Late fifteenth-century

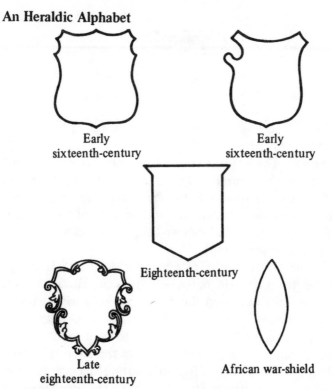

Early
sixteenth-century

Early
sixteenth-century

Eighteenth-century

Late
eighteenth-century

African war-shield

Shield of David (See **David, Shield of**)

Ship The stylized heraldic galley is the lymphad but a fleet of other vessels may be found. These are invariably detailed in the blazon. With sailing ships it is important to note not simply the type of ship but also whether the sails are furled and whether flags and pennons are flying. Normally a ship moves to the dexter so that the sails billow and the flags fly in that direction.

Shoveller Sometimes equated with the sheldrake, but although they are of the same family they are not of the same tribe and should be distinguished.

Shuttle The weaver's shuttle, which is prominent in the arms of many corporations in Lancashire and is also found in the canting coat of Shuttleworth. It is usually depicted as illustrated and is borne fesswise unless otherwise blazoned.

Shuttle

Silver The English word is sometimes used in place of argent to avoid repetition.

Sinister The left-hand side of the shield from the point of view of the bearer — the right as observed from the front. A charge qualified by the term sinister proceeds from or faces the sinister. The sinister side of the shield is the less important; the dexter taking precedence over it. (See **Points of the shield**)

Sir The titular prefix of a baronet or knight. It always precedes the Christian name or initials. In Tudor times it was sometimes accorded the clergy but only as a mark of respect.

Siren In some books this is said to be a synonym for mermaid but this is clearly wrong as the siren of Greek mythology was a very different creature, having the top half of a woman, the bottom half of a web-footed sea-bird and vast wings.

Sixfoil A six-leaved figure. Like the cinquefoil it can be pierced and in such form it occurs in the arms of Lambart, Earl of Cavan, although it is there blazoned as a 'narcissus'.

Skain (Also **Skean** and **Skene**) A Gaelic dagger. For an obvious reason the daggers in the arms of the family of Skene of that Ilk are usually blazoned 'skains'.

Slip A small twig, distinguished from a sprig or branch by bearing fewer — usually two or three — leaves.

Slipped Used of flowers and leaves, including stylized forms like the trefoil, which have stalks.

Snow flake This was not used in heraldry until the present century. It is blazoned a 'snow crystal' and a single, magnified crystal is shown. In the arms of Lord

Snow, which are simply 'azure, semy of snow crystals proper', stelliform crystals are depicted.

Sol Used for gold when blazoning by planets (See **Planets**)

Soleil (See **Rose-en-soleil**)

Somerset Herald The title of one of the six heralds in ordinary. Originally a private herald of Edmund Beaufort, Duke of Somerset, then in 1485 a royal herald. Later the title was given to the private herald of Henry VII's bastard son Henry Fitzroy, Duke of Richmond and Somerset. After his death Somerset became, and has remained, a royal herald. His badge is a gold portcullis with chains ensigned by the royal crown.

Southern cross This constellation, blazoned 'a representation of the Southern Cross', and properly symbolized by five mullets, one of eight, two of seven, one of six and one of five points, is frequently used in Antipodean coats of arms. Other representations are also found but that described above is now generally used.

Sovereignty, Arms of (See **Arms of Dominion**)

Spade Usually shown with a pointed shield-shaped end and strengthened with iron. The spade-iron is also found as a separate charge, as is a half-spade, that is a spade divided per pale, one half being shown.

Spancelled Used to describe a horse when a fore-leg and a hind-leg are fettered to a piece of wood.

Spear The tilting spear, but with a sharp point rather than a cronel, is usually depicted and is sometimes so blazoned. The spear-head is found as a separate charge.

Spear

Spear cronel   (See **Cronal**)

Sphere   (See **Globe** and **Celestial Sphere**)

Sperver   (also **Sparver**) A bed covering. (See **Tent**)

Sphinx   In mythology this monster has taken various forms but in heraldry the sphinx is normally shown with a lions's body and a woman's head and breasts, the head being draped in the Egyptian manner. Sometimes the Greek or winged sphinx is shown. Ford, baronet, has a winged sphinx as a crest, although as it holds a papyrus stalk it would seem that it is meant to allude to Egypt not Greece. If the position of a sphinx is not mentioned in the blazon it is usually safe to assume that it is couchant.

Sphinx

Spider's web   When a field is charged with a spider's web, the web is normally centred on the fess point, radiating outward.

Sprig   A small branch, normally having about five leaves attached to it. (See **Slip**)

Springing   A synonym for 'salient' but only used for deer and other beasts of the chase when in this position.

Spur   For obvious reasons the spur is frequently chosen as a charge by grantees who have received the accolade of knighthood. Unless specifically blazoned as a prickspur, the spur with rowel and strap (often of a different tincture from the spur) is depicted. It is always shown palewise and today the rowel is in chief, although this has not always been the case.

Spur Rowel   This is a pierced mullet. The word mullet, though now applied to an unpierced star, derives from the French *molette,* a spur rowel.

Square This refers not to the T-square but to the right-angled implement, one side being longer than the other, used by masons, carpenters and joiners. It is sometimes blazoned 'a carpenter's square'.

Square fretty (See **Fretty**)

Squirrel Unless otherwise blazoned, a squirrel is shown sejant erect. Frequently it holds a nut in its forepaws but if this is the case it should be specified in the blazon.

SS, Collar of The origin of this royal collar studded with esses, or composed of them linked together, is obscure. Originally worn by knights and esquires it is now only worn by kings of arms (in silver gilt) and heralds and serjeants at arms (in silver). The Lord Mayor of London and Lord Chief Justice also wear a form of this badge. King Henry IV is generally credited with devising this badge, S being the initial letter of his motto 'Souverayne' but there is now evidence to suggest a pre-fifteenth-century origin.

Collar of SS

Stag (See **Deer**)

Stains Sanguine, tenné and murrey are sometimes so called as they are often used in abatements which stain the nobility of the arms.

Stall plate A metal plate emblazoned with arms and used by knights of certain orders of chivalry, who place them over their stalls in the chapel of their order. Garter plates are in St George's Chapel, Windsor; Bath plates, erected by Knights Grand Cross of the Order of the Bath, are in King Henry VII's Chapel in Westminster Abbey, and so forth.

Standard   A long, tapering flag, originally split at the end. In the hoist or chief (that is the part next to the staff) was shown the cross of St George. Then in the fly, usually composed of the livery colours, was displayed the badge, motto on two diagonal bands and often also the crest. Round the flag was a parti-coloured fringe. The standard was the great rallying flag in the medieval battle, so when the feudal host gave way to the national army the personal standard had no further use and was carried only in funeral processions, the degree of the owner dictating the length of the flag. When the granting of personal badges to armigerous people was permitted by an Earl Marshal's Warrant in 1906, the standard, on which the badge featured prominently, was also revived. The new standards were in every way similar to the medieval forerunners except that the arms of the owner replaced the cross of St George in the hoist. Some Scottish standards still retain the cross of St Andrew in the hoist, whilst others display the personal coat of the owner. It should be noted that the royal standard is not in fact a standard but an elongated banner.

Modern standard

Ancient standard

Staple The type of staple illustrated is normally shown with points downwards unless otherwise blazoned.

Staple

Star The term 'star', once frequently used to blazon estoils, either irradiated or not, is not now employed. (See **Estoil** and **Mullet**)

Star of India, Order of the The Most Exalted Order of the Star of India was instituted in 1861. There are three classes: Knight Grand Commander, Knight Commander and Companion. All classes may suspend the appropriate insignia beneath their shield of arms and may surround it with the circle and motto. Holders of the first class are entitled to a grant of supporters and may place the collar of the order round their arms. As with the Order of the Indian Empire no appointments have been made to this order since 1947 and it may therefore be regarded as obsolescent.

Starved* (See **Blasted**)

Statant Used of animals when standing with all four feet on the ground.

Steps (See **Grieces**)

Stirrup If shown without the leather it is usually termed a stirrup iron, if with the leather then this should be intimated in the blazon.

Stock This is used to describe the stump of a tree, although the word 'stump' is also frequently found, and also the bar or timber of an anchor.

Stooping This is not an heraldic term so that when a bird of prey is so blazoned it is shown swooping on its prey as in nature.

Stork   (See **Heron**)

Strewed with   (also **Strewn with**) A synonym for 'semy' but not used in modern blazon.

Stringed   A term used when describing the strings of an instrument, such as the harp or lyre, the cord of a bugle horn or the string of a bow.

Sub-ordinaries   Diminutives of the ordinaries or geometrical charges of less importance. There seems little point in such a classification as the authors of textbooks seldom agree as to which charges shall be so designated. Apart from diminutives, the orle, tressure, double-tressure, canton, gyron, lozenge, fusil, muscle, rustre, fret, billet, inescutcheon, label, roundel and annulet are usually referred to as sub-ordinaries. Some writers give diminutives as a classification of their own, whilst others lump them in with either the ordinaries or sub-ordinaries.

Subverted*   (See **Reversed**)

Sufflue   (See **Clarion**)

Sun   The sun is normally depicted with rays alternately wavy and straight and with a human countenance. He is essentially masculine and is blazoned either simply 'a sun' or, more poetically a 'sun in (his) splendour' or 'in glory'. The former term is more usual. The number of rays and the addition of features is a matter of artistic treatment, although some families traditionally bear a certain type of sun.

Sun in splendour

Sunburst   The rays of the sun issuing from clouds. This was an ancient royal badge which today, ensigned by a royal crown, is the badge of Windsor Herald.

Super-charge Sometimes used to describe a charge which surmounts another.

Supporters Figures placed on either side of a shield to support it. They were first used, albeit capriciously, by some great magnates in the fifteenth century but their systematized use is from the mid-sixteenth century. Today supporters are granted only to peers of the realm, Knights of the Garter, Thistle and St Patrick, and to knights of the first class of the various orders of chivalry and the Order of St John. Such supporters are personal to the grantee except in the case of hereditary peers, where the supporters are inherited with the peerage. The eldest son of a peer, even though he may use one of his father's junior titles, has no right to use the supporters until he inherits. Supporters are also granted to certain corporations. Although this is done to a great extend on an *ad hoc* basis, the following classes of corporation are not normally denied the privilege of supporters: county, city and borough councils, the London livery companies, nationalized bodies and bodies incorporated by royal charter. In Scotland supporters may be granted at will by Lord Lyon King of Arms but in fact he assigns them very sparingly. Certain minor barons, knights and clan chiefs may claim them by right and the heir-apparent to a man having supporters may, in Scotland, use these. There are some ancient families in both England and Scotland who claim a right to supporters although not qualifying under the present rules and there are also some to whom supporters have been granted by virtue of a special royal warrant. Almost any animate being may be used as a supporter, although some are obviously more suitable than others and there are even recent examples of inanimate supporters, like the garbs which support, or at least are supported by, the arms of Lord Boyd-Orr.

Suppressed (See **Debruised**)

Surcoat A long coat, also termed the coat armour,

which was worn over the armour. Surcoats first appear in the middle of the twelfth century and towards the end of the thirteenth century. Examples of them emblazoned with arms are to be found on effigies. By the middle of the fourteenth century the surcoat had given way to the skirted armorial jupon, the skirts of which gradually grew briefer until, after about 1430, apart from an occasional heraldic tabard, all forms of material covering the armour were discarded.

Surjeant* (Also **Surgiant**) Used to describe a bird rising from the ground.

Surmounted (See **Debruised**)

Surtout (See **Over all**)

Swan When a swan is gorged with a coronet and chained it is sometimes termed a 'cygnet royal'. The term 'swan's neck' comprehends both neck and head.

Swastika Called a 'fylfot' or 'cross gamadion' in heraldry. (See **Cross**)

Swepe Another name for the mangonel or balista, an ancient siege engine, which is sometimes found in armory.

Sword Unless a specific variety of sword is detailed in the blazon it is usual to show a long, straight-bladed sword, with crosspiece and grip ending in a pommel. Unless well drawn it is often difficult to distinguish between a sword and a dagger, only the blazon giving the clue.

Sword

Syke (See **Fountain**)

Tabard The loose surcoat which superseded the jupon in the first half of the fifteenth century. The word was originally applied to the frock earlier worn by peasants. The armorial tabard was emblazoned with arms on the front, back and on either sleeve and it is likely that heralds first wore cast-off tabards given them by their master as a mark of their special relationship to him. The tabard continued to be the distinctive garb of a herald after it had been abandoned, first as an actual garment and later as a symbolic garment carried in funeral processions. Today kings of arms wear velvet, heralds satin and pursuivants damask-silk tabards embroidered with the royal arms. Scottish heralds wear tabards of the royal arms as used in Scotland. Originally pursuivants used to wear their tabards athwart but since about James II's reign they have worn them the right way round.

Tabard

Talbot The heraldic dog. It has a mastiff's body with hound's head and bloodhound's long drooping ears.

Talbot statant

Talent Originally a weight, later a coin and so a

synonym for a bezant.

Targe (also **Target**) Usually applied to a circular shield with a centre boss but also used to describe the heraldic shield borne at a man's funeral.

Tass (See **Potent**)

Tassel When a charge has tassels attached to it, for example a cushion with tassels at each corner, it is blazoned as being tasselled. Tassels are often attached to the mantling and in sixteenth century grants their presence was usually mentioned, as in the grant to John Shakespeare, but today they are regarded as an artistic embellishment and are invariably painted gold, although there would seem to be no convention, other than custom, for so depicting them.

Tassy Vairy (also **Tass Vairy**) (See **Potent**)

Taw Cross (See **Cross**)

Tawny (See **Tenné**)

Tenné (also **Tenny, Tawny, Orange** or **Busk**) Tawny-orange colour. Although accorded many names by heraldic writers I can find no example of the use of this stain in English armory until the twentieth century when, like murrey and sanguine, it has enjoyed a measure of popularity. In engraving, horizontal lines crossed by diagonal lines in bend sinister are used to indicate tenné.

Tent Unless some particular blazon or tradition dictates otherwise, a circular tent with centre pole visible between the open tent-flaps is normally depicted. In the arms of the Merchant Taylors' Company of London the circular tent in the arms is called a 'pavillion imperial' whilst those in the Upholders' Company of London's arms, though almost identical in shape, are blazoned 'spervers'; the sperver or sparver being a tent-like bed covering.

Tergiant* Turned so that the back faces outwards.

Terrestrial globe (See **Globe**)

Theow (also **Thoye**) A wolf-like monster but with a cow's tail and cloven hooves. It is a beast of the Cheyne family.

Theow

Thistle Usually drawn slipped and leaved in a some-what stylized and formal manner.

Thistle

Thistle, Order of the The Most Ancient and Most Noble Order of the Thistle has traditional origins back in the eighth century but it was revived in 1687 by King James II and later revised by Queen Anne in 1703 and King George IV in 1827. It consists of the sovereign and sixteen knights. These are entitled to a grant of supporters, to encircle their arms with the collar, circle and motto of the order and to suspend the badge beneath the arms. Lyon King of Arms is the king of arms and secretary of the order. The chapel of the order is in St Giles Cathedral, Edinburgh, and here may be seen the banners and stall plates of the knights.

Thoye (See **Theow**)

Throughout (also **Entire**) When a charge whose extremities do not normally reach the edges of the shield is shown in such a way, it is blazoned 'throughout'.

Thunderbolt A charge taken from classical mythology.

It consists of a flaming winged column with four rays of lightning in saltire.

Thunderbolt

Thyrsus In classical mythology this was the staff carried by Dionysus (or in Italy, Bacchus) and his attendants. It usually consisted of a pointed rod entwined with vine leaves and with a pine-cone at the top. A rather emasculated thyrsus was included in the arms granted to Henry Sissmore in 1796, the grape vine becoming ivy.

Thyrsus

Tiara This normally refers to the triple papal crown, rather than the diadem worn by ladies on high days.

Tierced (also **Triparted**) An Anglicization of the French term 'tiercé' meaning divided into three. In English blazon its use seems to be confined to a shield 'tierced in pairle' or 'in pairle reversed'. This way of dividing the field is comparatively recent, which is perhaps why this rather clumsy term has been imported from the continent rather than employing a new but obvious term, 'per pall'.

Tierced
in pairle

Tiger (See **Tyger**)
Tilting spear (See **Spear**)
Timbre* (also **Tymbre**) The crest.

Tinctures This term refers to all the colours, metals and furs in the heraldic paint-box. The two metals are or (gold) and argent (silver). The five colours are gules (red), azure (blue), sable (black), vert (green) and purpure (purple). The three lesser colours, sometimes called stains and used but infrequently, are murrey (mulberry-colour), sanguine (blood-red) and tenne (tawny-orange). The furs are ermine (black ermine spots on white), ermines (the reverse), erminois (black spots on gold) and pean (the reverse). Vair is a fur consisting of alternate blue and white pelts; vairy is pelts of diverse tinctures which must, of course, be named in the blazon. In vair en point and counter-vair the pellets are arranged in a different manner from usual. Potent is accorded the distinction of being a fur but is really only vair drawn differently; counter-potent, likewise, is a variation of potent. In engraving the tinctures are indicated by a system of shading (see **Hatching**). For details of the various tinctures see under the separate headings.

Tines (also **Tynes**) The points on the antlers of a stag. Usually the number is indefinite but five are commonly shown. This is curious as the royal stag has six points on each antler (brow, bez, trez and three tops).

Topaz Used for or when blazoning by jewels. (See **Jewels**)

Torch The torch of classical antiquity is always depicted and it is usually blazoned as a 'torch enflamed'. The torch is sometimes found winged.

Torch

Torqued Wreathed.

Torse (See **Wreath**)

Torteau Term applied to a roundel when it is red. Many textbooks state that the torteau should be shaded to look spherical but there seems to be no basis for this statement. In French blazon all coloured roundels are called *torteaux* (we use the same plural in English blazon) but if they are spherical they are termed *boules*.

Tourné (See **Contourné**)

Tower A single battlemented tower, usually with a port at the base. It should not be confused with a castle. When three small turrets issue from the top of a tower it is blazoned a 'tower triple-towered' or 'triple-turreted'.

Tower
triple-towered

Tragopan According to Pliny a tragopan is essentially an eagle with curved horns. Although no actual blazon exists this monster is clearly that granted to Robert Laward, alias Lord, in the early 16th century.

Transfixed Pierced right through. (See **Pierced**)

Transfluent Flowing through; used to describe water flowing under a bridge.

Traversed* Facing the sinister.

Tree Many varieties of tree are found in heraldry and the number is constantly increasing as more and more coats of arms are granted to individuals and corporations in distant parts of the Commonwealth; naturally they often favour the flora, and fauna also, of their various countries. Trees, therefore, are usually drawn as in nature but often the older heraldic trees, such as the oak, are drawn in a stylized way with large leaves and fruit. However no distinction is made in the blazon. If the roots of a tree are shown it is said to be 'eradicated'.

Treflé The cross botonny (see **Cross**) is sometimes called a cross treflé. The term is also used of charges adorned with trefoils or semy of trefoils.

Trefoil A three-leaved figure resembling a clover leaf. It is generally shown slipped at the base but this fact is usually stated in the blazon.

Trefoil

Tressure A diminutive of the orle. It is usually, but not invariably, shown double and flory-counterflory. (See **Double-tressure**)

Trian Aspect, in* A textbook term referring to a beast which is half-way between the passant and afronty positions.

Triangle When this occurs in arms, which is but infrequently, an equilateral triangle is shown. (See **David, Shield of**)

Trick A method of indicating the tinctures of a coat of arms by the use of abbreviations. The common abbreviations used in tricking arms are g. or gu. (gules); b. (i.e. blue) or, rarely, az. – it can be confused with ar. – (azure); s. or sa. (sable); v. or vt. (vert); purp. (purpure); o. or written in full (or); a. or ar. (argent) and ppr. (proper).

Tricorporate   Having three bodies radiating from one central head. A lion tricorporate is a known charge.

Lion tricorporate

Trident   A three-pronged spear. Neptune usually carries one.

Trillium flower   A recent but welcome addition to the heraldic garden. It has been used principally in Canadian arms.

Trillium flower

Trinity   The ancient symbol of the Holy Trinity, sometimes called the 'shield of the Trinity'. It often forms the arms attributed to churches dedicated to the Trinity; it is also occasionally used in official armory.

Trinity

Triparted (See **Tierce**)

Trippant Used in palce of passant when describing beasts of the deer variety when in this position. 'Counter-trippant' is likewise a synonym for 'counter-passant'. (See **Counter**)

Triquetra Three equal interlaced arcs. Normally used as a symbol of the Blessed Trinity.

Triquetra

Triton In classical mythology Triton was the son of Poseidon and Amphitrite and lived beneath the water. He was represented as a man with a dolphin's tail usually holding a twisted sea shell, which is how he is depicted in heraldry.

Triumphal crown A wreath or crown of laurel.

Trogodice A creature similar to a reindeer but with long horns curving forwards.

Trogodice

Troncone* Couped at all the joints.

True-love-knot (or **True lovers' knot**) A knot of ribbon, usually blue, which sometimes surmounts, as an artistic conceit, the lozenge of a spinster.

Trumpet A simple long horn is usually represented but there are examples of more sophisticated trumpets.

Trussed* A bird with closed wings.

Trussing Sometimes used to describe a bird devouring its prey.

Tudor rose (See **Rose**)

Tufted A term used to refer to the tufts of hair on animals' tails, limbs, etc. when of a different tincture from the body. (See **Crined**)

Tun A barrel. It is frequently used in the arms and rebuses of those whose names end in 'ton'.

Turkey Like the peacock the turkey is frequently shown 'in his pride' with tail fanned. William Strickland is supposed to have brought the first turkey from North America to England and his crest, granted in 1550, is a turkey cock; certainly it is the first in English heraldry.

Turkey cock crest
of Strickland

Turned* (See **Doubled**)

Turned up Used of chapeaux when describing the lining which is turned up so as to show round the edge.

Turret A small tower emanating from the top of a large tower.

Twyfoil* (See **Unifoil**)

Tyger (also **Tiger**) The heraldic tyger is a strange beast. It has a lion's body (no stripes), tufts, pointed ears, tusks and a sort of beak at the end of its nose. When those who had seen service in India wanted a tiger in their arms, they were not content with the traditional, symbolic beast; they demanded the true *felis tigris*, and the splendid Bengal variety at that, so the natural tiger is now called a 'Bengal tiger' (unless he definitely hails from elsewhere) and the tyger is sometimes, but quite unnecessarily if the archaic spelling is used, called the 'heraldic tyger'.

Tyger

Tynes (See **Tines**)

Ulster King of Arms The title of the former principal herald of all Ireland. The office was instituted by King Edward VI in 1552-3. His office was at Dublin Castle and when the Order of St Patrick was instituted in 1783 he became the Registrar and Knight Attendant. His official arms were: 'or, a cross gules, on a chief of the last, a lion passant guardant between a harp and a portcullis, all or.' In 1943 the office was merged with that of Norroy King of Arms.

Umbre, En (See **Adumbration**)

Undy (also **Undé** or **Ondé**) A synonym for wavy. It is not much used today but in early blazon it was always employed, often meaning barry wavy. (See **Partition, Lines of**)

Unguled Although the Latin word *ungula* from which this adjective is derived means claw, talon or hoof, in heraldry the term 'unguled' is confined to describing the hoofs of animals when of a different tincture from their bodies.

Unicorn One of the most popular and ancient monsters in heraldry. It is usually drawn as a horse with a single long twisted horn, lion's tail and the legs and cloven hoofs of a stag.

Unicorn

Unifoil Said to look like the single leaf of a trefoil but one has yet to be discovered outside the textbooks. If it has two leaves it is said to be a twyfoil but this too seems to be a figment of the imagination of an heraldic writer.

Union Flag Commonly called the Union Jack, this flag has come to be regarded as the national flag of the United Kingdom of Great Britain and Northern Ireland, although properly it is a government and naval flag. The saltire of St Andrew and cross of St George were first jointed into one flag in 1606 to be worn by all ships 'in their fore-toppe'. In 1634 the Union, of which no picture or blazon was officially recorded, was confined to ships of the Royal Navy. In 1707, on the union of England and Scotland, a new flag was proclaimed and recorded. It consisted of the saltire of St Andrew on a blue field with the St George's cross over all, fimbriated argent. This flag persisted until the union with Ireland in 1801 when the present Union Flag was proclaimed. It is blazoned 'azure, the crosses saltire of St Andrew and St Patrick, quarterly per saltire counter-changed argent and gules, the latter fimbriated of the second, surmounted by the cross of St George of the third, fimbriated as the saltire'.

Union flag

Urchin (also **Urcheon**) The usual heraldic name for a hedgehog. It is also called a herisson or herizon as in the canting arms of some families of Harris.

Urdy (also **Urdé** and **Aiguise**) (See **Cross** and **Partition, Lines of**)

Urinal Although this charge fortunately occurs but once in English armory, namely as the crest granted to Dr Louys Caerlyon in 1483 ('an urinal in its cage proper') it is so unlike what is commonly understood today by the word urinal that it is perhaps worth illustrating.

Urinal crest of Caerlyon

Urinant (also **Uriant**) Term applied to a fish when diving with head downwards and belly to the sinister.

Use arms (See **Bear arms**)

User (See **Ancient user**)

Vair One of the two principal furs used in heraldry. It consists of small animals' skins joined together head to tail. In early armory it was drawn like joined cups (sometimes called 'vair ancient') but later the pelts were drawn like ugly shields with 'ears' and a pointed base (occasionally referred to as 'vair en point'). When the skins are arranged top to top and tail to tail it is termed 'vair counter', or 'counter vair'. Pedants call vair composed of small skins 'menu vair' and that formed from large skins 'gros vair', but these terms are not used in blazon. The skins are always alternately argent and azure. If vair consists of any other two or more tinctures, then it is blazoned 'vairé' or 'vairy' of the tinctures in question. (See **Potent**)

| Vair (ancient form) | Vair (modern form) | Counter vair |

Vairé (also **Vairy**) (See **Vair**)

Vallary Crown A crown consisting of a number (usually eight, four being visible) of pointed projections rising from a rim. It is similar to a palisado crown. (See **Crown**)

Vambraced Although the vambrace was fore-arm armour, the term vambraced is used to denote an arm completely encased in armour.

Vamplate The wide part of a tilting spear which protects the hand of the holder.

Vane A synonym for a fan but it is also used to describe a small flag, which is the original meaning of the word in Old English. It is also an abbreviation of the term 'weather vane'. (See **Fan**)

Vannet* An escallop minus the projecting ears. A

textbook term. Possibly it originally meant a small fan, which resembles an escallop in outline.

Veined A term which refers to the veins of a leaf when of a different tincture from the leaf itself. 'Nerved' is another but rarer term.

Varvel The ring or swivel at the end of a hawk's jess. (See **Jess**)

Venus Used for vert when blazoning by planets. (See **Planets**)

Verdoy Employed when blazoning a bordure charged with flowers, leaves or similar charges. It is rarely used but is still found in Scottish blazon.

Vert The colour green. In engraving diagonal lines in bend are used to indicate vert. It is abbreviated $v.$ or $vt.$ and is pronounced as spelt.

Vested Clothed. Another word often used is 'habited'.

Vicar Apostolic (See **Protonotary Apostolic**)

Victoria Cross A decoration instituted in 1856 to signalize special individual acts of bravery. A representation of it may be suspended beneath the shield.

Victorian Chain, Royal This was instituted by King Edward VII in 1902 and is bestowed only on special occasions, many of those who now have it being foreign heads of state. It is not part of the Royal Victorian Order. As the chain may be worn when decorations are worn, presumably it may also encircle the shield of arms, but as there are no statutes this remains a matter for speculation.

Victorian Order, Royal The Royal Victorian Order was instituted in 1896 and has since been revised and enlarged on various occasions. There are five classes: 1 Knight and Dame Grand Cross, 2 Knight and Dame Commander, 3 Commander, 4 Member of the 4th Class and 5 Member of the 5th Class.

All classes suspend the appropriate insignia beneath their arms and the first three classes surround their arms with the circle and motto of the order. Holders of the first class are entitled to a grant of supporters and may place the collar of the order round their arms. The chapel of the order is the Chapel of the Savoy.

Vigilance (See **Heron**)

Virols The bands which encircle a horn. (See **Bugle Horn**)

Viscount The fourth rank in the peerage. The first viscount to be created in England was John Beaumont in 1440. (See **Peer**)

Viscountess The title of the wife of a viscount or that of a woman who holds a viscouncy in her own right.

Visitations The name given to the periodic visitations of the counties of England made by the kings of arms or their deputies by virtue of a royal commission. These commissions were issued at more or less regular intervals between 1530 and 1686, the purpose being to record the arms and pedigrees of the gentry, deface arms improperly or unlawfully used and denounce those who bore arms without authority. During the visitation period most counties were visited about five times and the resultant records provide an invaluable source of genealogical and armorial material.

Visor (also **Vizor**) The moveable face-covering on a helmet. The position of the visor of the helmet in an achievement of arms indicates the rank of the bearer. Gentlemen, esquires and corporations have closed visors and their helmets face the dexter; knights and baronets have open visors and their helmets face the front. Peers and royalty have barred helms. (See **Helmet**)

Voided A term meaning that the middle of a charge has been cut out, allowing the field or another tincture to show through.

Voider A synonym for, or possibly a diminutive of 'the flaunch'.

Vol Two wings conjoined in lure with tips upwards. A single wing is called a demi-vol. This is really a French term and is certainly not now used in blazon. (See **Wing**)

Volant A bird flying is termed volant. Normally it will

be facing the dexter and will have its legs drawn up to distinguish it from a bird rising or rousant. In old blazon 'volant' was simply a synonym for 'rising'.

Voluted A synonym for 'encircled' when applied to serpents. (See **Encircled**)

Vorant Devouring.

Vulned Wounded and disgorging blood. A creature vulned with an arrow or similar weapon is shown with it sticking into the body. If it should pierce the body then it would have to be blazoned as 'pierced by' or 'transfixed by' the weapon.

Vulning (See **Pelican**)

Wake knot (See **Knot**)

Wallet (See **Palmer's staff**)

War cry The war cry or *cri de guerre* is often used as a motto by ancient families, sometimes in addition to a later and more placid aphorism. In such cases one is placed beneath the shield, the other above the crest.

Water This is represented by barry wavy argent and azure but it is sometimes also found in its natural form. Although both symbolic and natural water are sometimes blazoned 'proper', the symbolic variety is more frequently blazoned 'water barry wavy argent and azure', the exact number of wavy bars sometimes being detailed. Obviously it is only sensible to draw a distinction in blazon between 'water proper' and 'water barry wavy argent and azure'.

Water-bouget (also **Water-budget**) A symbolic representation of a yoke supporting two leather water-bags. It is an ancient charge, in medieval times being associated with the family of Bourchier, and it is depicted in a variety of ways although no distinction in blazon is made between its different forms.

Forms of
water-bouget

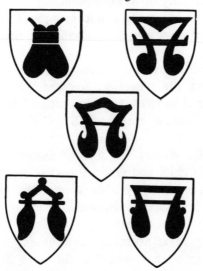

Wattled   Refers to the wattles of a cock. (See **Jelloped**)

Waves of the sea   When this phrase occurs in a blazon it usually means that natural waves should be shown but sometimes 'barry wavy argent and azure' is used. (See **Water**)

Wavy   (See **Partition, Lines of**)

Weare   (See **Weel**)

Weather vane   There is no stylized way in which this object should be drawn. It is also found simply blazoned 'vane'. Textbooks usually equate it with a weather cock but it would seem sensible to reserve this term for when an actual cock is shown.

Weel   (also **Weare, Fish weel** and **Fish weare**) A type of basket used for catching fish. There are several examples of its use in heraldry but it is depicted in various ways and given a variety of names.

Welke   (See **Whelk**)

Well   Although wells are often symbolized by the fountain, actual wells do occur in armory and are usually depicted as circular structures of masonry viewed in perspective from slightly above. In this form they occur in the arms of the City of Wells in Somerset.

Wheat   This is usually found in a sheaf, called a garb, but single ears or a specified number of ears occur. (See **Big**)

Wheel   This is usually represented by an eight-spoked cartwheel, but the wheel in the arms of a family of Brymer, granted in 1814, has a rim rather like a cog-wheel, although it is not so blazoned. (See **Catherine wheel** and **Cog wheel**)

Whelk   (also **Welke**) The shell of the whelk erect, with the opening in chief and with no part of the fish visible is normally understood by this term. The more precise expression 'whelk shell' is also used.

Whirlpool   (See **Gurges**)

White   Argent is normally represented by white, and some will argue that when a fur such as ermine is represented, the use of white, rather than silver, is obligatory.

Whelk

White Ensign (See **Ensign**)

Wild man (See **Savage**)

Windsor Herald The title of one of the six heralds in ordinary. It is one of the oldest titles now in use, probably dating back to as early as 1338. It has been employed consistently since the early fifteenth century. His badge is a sunburst ensigned by the royal crown.

Wing Unless the blazon specifies otherwise the stylized dexter wing of the eagle is usually depicted with tip to the chief. When two wings are joined with tips downwards they are said to be 'conjoined in lure'. Crests are often depicted between two wings. In such cases the wings are sometimes shown addorsed and sometime displayed, although the blazon does not always differentiate between these two position. (See **In lure** and **Vol**)

Winged Having wings attached. Ordinary beasts can be made into monsters by the addition of wings. The winged lion, horse (pegasus), stag and bull are no strangers to heraldry. Equally, wingless monsters can be made more monstrous by the addition of wings, as witness winged sea-stags, winged sea-lions and winged unicorns.

Winnowing fan (See **Fan**)

Wodehouse (also **Woodhouse**, **Woodwose** and similar) A wild man of the woods, generally depicted as bearded and covered in green hair except for the face, elbows, knees, hands and feet, where the flesh is visible.

Wodehouse

Wool pack This looks like a roughly made cushion. The corners are tied but the resultant 'ears' often resemble the more sophisticated tassels of the cushion.

Women's arms Women are entitled to bear their father's arms in a lozenge but without helmet, mantling or crest. There is some artistic licence as to how the lozenge, which is a harsh, unlovely shape, may be depicted. Often a true lover's knot is shown at the top of the lozenge. At one time women were denied mottoes (except in Scottish heraldry) but this is not now the case. When a woman marries, her husband incorporates her arms with his own, impaling them if she is not an heiress or placing them on an escutcheon of pretence if she is. A widow continues to bear the marital coat but in a lozenge. A woman may use insignia and, if entitled to them, bear supporters. A divorced woman reverts to her maiden arms, but charged with a mascle for distinction and borne upon a lozenge. Women do not have marks of cadency unless, being members of the royal family, they are granted them by the sovereign.

A woman not being an heiress but being a grantee of arms may transmit her arms, impaled by those of her husband and all within a bordure of a suitable tincture, as a quartering to her descendants in the usual manner.

| Arms of an unmarried woman | Arms of husband and wife | Arms of a divorced woman |

Wreath (also **Torse**) The strands of material twisted and wreathed about the base of the crest where it is affixed to the helmet. The blazon of a crest encircled by a wreath invariably begins: 'On a wreath of the colours . . . ' The preposition 'on' is misleading, for the crest ought to issue forth from the wreath and should not, as eighteenth and nineteenth-century heraldic painters were wont to portray it, sit on the wreath. Fifteenth- and early sixteenth-century blazons frequently describe the crest and then add some expression such as 'sett within a wreath' (from a grant made in 1478), which seems a more descriptive phrase. The wreath now normally consists of six (visible) twists. When it is said to be 'of the colours' it means that it is composed of the principal metal and tincture of the arms. From the end of the sixteenth century until the accession of Queen Elizabeth II the use of a wreath of the colours has been the general practice. However, in early- and pre-Tudor days this convention was seldom observed and during the reign of the present Queen there has been a return to earlier practice, and wreaths of different tinctures from the principal ones in the arms, and also of more than two tinctures, are frequently granted. The wreath is sometimes used as a charge, in which case it is shown in the form of a ring. As a verb it is employed to describe a charge which is 'wreathed about' with any sort of garland or torse. An ordinary can be shown 'wreathed' as is the fess in the arms of Carmichael or the bend 'cotised wreathy' granted to the Rev. William Rose in 1781 and illustrated here.

Bend cotised wreathy

Wyvern   (also **Wivern**) This monster resembles a dragon in every respect except that it has no hind-quarters, its rear being like that of a serpent with barbed tail. (See **Dragon**)

Wyvern

Yale (also **Eale** and **Jall**) Representations of this monster, called $\breve{e}\bar{a}l\bar{e}$ by Pliny, vary. Its principal attributes are large tusks and long, usually curved horns which it can swivel at will. For the rest the yale sometimes has a body like an antelope's with a lion's tail, as in the 'Bedford Book of Hours' where it is a supporter of the arms of John, Duke of Bedford (died 1435), and sometimes it is a more thickset beast with a goat's tail. The yales on the roof of St George's Chapel, Windsor, have the hind-paws of a lion, but in this they would appear to be unique

Yale

Yellow Frequently used in painting arms to represent gold.

Ypotryll An unpleasant and rare monster. It appears to have a face like a boar's with tusks, the body of a camel with two hairy humps, and the legs, hooves and mane of an ox. It was probably a badge of John Tiptoft, Earl of Worcester (died 1471).

York Herald The title of one of the six heralds in ordinary. York Herald is first mentioned in the time of Edward IV, from which period the title has been consistently employed. His badge is a white rose en soleil ensigned by the royal crown.

Zodiac, Signs of the The astronomical signs of the Zodiac are sometimes used as charges.

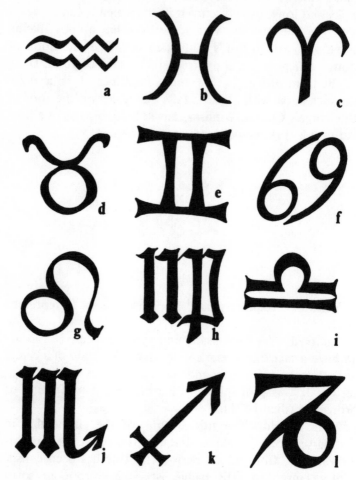

Signs of the Zodiac
a) Aquarius b) Pisces c) Aries d) Taurus e) Gemini
f) Cancer g) Leo h) Virgo
i) Libra j) Scorpio k) Sagittarius l) Capricornus

Zule (See **Chess rook**)